D0684990

ONE
KINGDOM
UNDER
GOD

THE LIFE UNDER GOD SERIES

ONE KINGDOM UNDER GOD

His Rule Over All

TONY EVANS

MOODY PUBLISHERS

CHICAGO

© 2014 by
ANTHONY T. EVANS

All rights reserved. No part of this book may be reproduced in any form without permission in writing from the publisher, except in the case of brief quotations embodied in critical articles or reviews.

Some of the content of this book has been adapted from *The Kingdom Agenda* by Tony Evans ©2013.

All Scripture quotations, unless otherwise indicated, are taken from the *New American Standard Bible*®, Copyright © 1960, 1962, 1963, 1968, 1971, 1972, 1973, 1975, 1977, 1995 by The Lockman Foundation. Used by permission. (www.Lockman.org)

Scripture quotations marked NIV are taken from the *Holy Bible, New International Version*®, NIV®. Copyright © 1973, 1978, 1984, 2011 by Biblica, Inc.™ Used by permission of Zondervan. All rights reserved worldwide. www.zondervan.com. The "NIV" and "New International Version" are trademarks registered in the United States Patent and Trademark Office by Biblica, Inc.™

Interior design: Erik M. Peterson
Cover design: Smartt Guys design
Cover image: Konstantin Sutyagin / Shutterstock

Library of Congress Cataloging-in-Publication Data

Evans, Tony, 1949-
  One kingdom under God : His rule over all / Tony Evans.
    pages cm
  ISBN 978-0-8024-1189-1
  1. Kingdom of God. I. Title.
  BT94.E85 2014
  231.7'2—dc23
                      2014011573

We hope you enjoy this book from Moody Publishers. Our goal is to provide high-quality, thought-provoking books and products that connect truth to your real needs and challenges. For more information on other books and products written and produced from a biblical perspective, go to www.moodypublishers.com or write to:

Moody Publishers
820 N. LaSalle Boulevard
Chicago, IL 60610

1 3 5 7 9 10 8 6 4 2

Printed in the United States of America

CONTENTS

INTRODUCTION

The kingdom agenda is God's blueprint for how life ought to be lived. It needs to remain at the forefront of our thinking in order to fully penetrate our choices and decisions, thus bringing about the full realization of its covenantal blessings and authority.

Unfortunately, it seems the message of the kingdom is sorely lacking today. This is not because people don't speak of the kingdom, but because far too much of their speech is in esoteric, theological code words that seem unrelated to the realities of life in the here-and-now.

The absence of a comprehensive agenda for life has led to deterioration of cosmic proportions in our world. People live segmented, compartmentalized lives because they lack a kingdom worldview. Families disintegrate because they exist for their own fulfillment rather than for the kingdom.

Churches are having a limited impact on society because they fail to understand the goal of the church is not the church itself, but the kingdom. This myopic perspective keeps the church divided, ingrown, and unable to transform the cultural landscape in any long-term, significant way.

Because of this, society at large has nowhere to turn to find solid solutions to the perplexing challenges that confront us today—troubling problems such as crime, racism, injustice, family disintegration, poverty, and myriad other ills.

The hope we so desperately look for in our lives, families, churches, and nation, will only come by way of living all of life under God's kingdom agenda. We need to align our lives under an agenda that is a comprehensive demonstration of the way our Creator intended every area of life to function. We need an agenda big enough to include both individuals and societal structures, clear enough to be understood and appropriated by the average person on the street, yet flexible enough to allow for the considerable differences among peoples and societies.

The kingdom agenda provides this path: a way to see and live life in this world. Such an agenda can hold its own against any of the humanistic worldviews of our day. It transcends the politics of men and offers the solutions of heaven.

OUR FASCINATION WITH KINGDOM

Cradled within the depths that define our humanity lies an unyielding fascination with kingdom. No matter what color, creed, or culture we examine, we find—with the most cursory glance into the annals and accounts passed down by either pen or tongue—something intertwined with kingdom.

Whether it be the great kings and rulers of Scripture such as David or Solomon, or whether it be Caesar, Alexander the Great, Charlemagne, Tutankhamen and the like, these lives somehow captivate us, intriguing our imaginations.

Even rulers who did not hold the official title of king have left their legacies to enthrall us, for good or for bad. There is Napoleon, the dominator of continental Europe, who possessed a formidable intellect and superior military mind. There is Khan, the evil and brutal ruler, who conquered most of the world during his time. There are the pharaohs, most of whom possessed such strength and skill that, for many centuries, their nations surpassed others in academics, engineering, medicine, and writing. Then there are also the monarchs spanning over 1600 years of history, in one form or fashion, beginning humbly as the Angles, moving to Aengla Land, and eventually becoming what we know it as today, England.

Stories of conquerors, conquests, rebellions, and conspiracy mesmerize us. We tell them to our children in fairy tales riddled with kings, queens, princes, princesses, and kingdoms. We read about them in history books, mythology, fables, legends, and fiction. We flock to movies to watch the rise or fall of power connected to a kingdom in epic adventures. Inevitably, we portray the king or the prince as reputedly handsome—when he is a good king. We portray him as sinister and ugly when he is bad.

Queens and princesses alike do not get lost from playing out a role in our fascination. From Cinderella to Nefertiti to Elizabeth I, we hold in highest regard that special strength of a woman who both utilizes and maintains her nobility, in the face of constant and devastating betrayal and opposition, in order to produce a greater good for her kingdom and her subjects.

The life of a king or queen is often envied. Yet, envy is naïve. Any true historian knows the utter fragility that comes with absolute power. As the playwright Shakespeare once wrote, "Uneasy lies the head that wears the crown." Kings, queens, and rulers frequently function in a culture of conflict and even violence. Those around them might swear an oath of total allegiance while simultaneously plotting their destruction.

As a result, history reminds us again and again through what may seem like the same story—just set on a different stage—that kings and rulers often resort to brute force and extreme taxation to protect their own personal interests and power. While uprisers such as the likes of the Scottish William Wallace (best known for being portrayed in *Braveheart*) could wind up hung and quartered in a meat factory, it wasn't only the uprisers who needed to fear the paranoid wrath that sometimes appeared in a king. No one was safe when it came to the possibility of usurping his role, as we see with the myriad instances of poisoning of family members, siblings, and even the gruesome, bloody beheading of wives with Henry VIII.

Nowhere in any story of a king or in any story of a kingdom do we read about the ruler himself sacrificing his own greatest treasure simply for the benefit of others. Sure, sacrifices were made. Lives were lost. But always toward the aim of preserving power, rather than yielding it. Except for the one, true King of the Bible who gave up His own Son, Jesus Christ, in order that those who believe on Him—His death, burial, and resurrection—would be restored to the place of both fellowship and dominion with their King—something they had lost in the Battle of the Garden.

THE UNUSUAL KINGDOM

It is not unusual that this unusual action occurred by this very unusual King, because His is an even more unusual kingdom. Jesus spoke of it plainly when He told Pilate the ways of His kingdom do not reflect the ways of the kingdoms on earth, "My kingdom is not of this world." He said, "If it were, my servants would fight to prevent my arrest by the Jewish leaders. But now my kingdom is from another place" (John 18:36 NIV). When His followers asked Him who was the greatest in this unusual kingdom, Jesus pulled a child close to Him and replied, "Therefore, whoever takes the lowly position of this child is the greatest in the kingdom of heaven." And then, continuing—rather than requiring and demanding the pomp and circumstance typically befit for a king—He instructed His subjects on how He would like to be approached as their Ruler and Lord, "And whoever welcomes one such child in my name," Jesus said, "welcomes me" (Matthew 18:4, 5 NIV).

This is a kingdom without borders and a kingdom without time. To try and apply the rules, precepts, and writs of this world to this unearthly kingdom would be similar to bringing a linebacker on a football field a horse and a polo stick and instructing him to get on with it, and play. The rules and tools of this earth do not govern the rules of God's kingdom. As King, He sets the way it is to both operate and function.

In His kingdom, neither race nor gender delineates inequality. In His kingdom, power goes to the weak who recognize their weakness and humbly look to Him. Forgiveness reigns preeminently, and the amount of money matters less than the heart that offers it, as we see in the case of the widow and her mite. Significance, in this unusual kingdom, is connected to service. Hope comes through helping others who may need it.

That is not to say there are no battles to fight or wars to win in this kingdom, or that this is a kingdom of rainbows, waterfalls, and unending bliss. There is a vile enemy still lurking and still seeking to dethrone the King of this kingdom, because this kingdom is the greatest kingdom of all and will also last the longest—just like it began before any others had.

Before there ever was an earth, there was a kingdom. This kingdom existed solely in the heavenlies, and it was a place of glory, majesty, and beauty. Yet treason was committed in an attempt to steal the seat of power, and those caught in an attempt to lay siege to the throne were repudiated—kicked down into darkness, which would later be sculpted and called Earth. Satan, the leader of this primeval rebellion, now uses charm, deception, distraction, temptation, lust, pride, apathy, evil, and all else to try to establish a rival kingdom whose subjects aim to defeat the subjects of the one, true King.

Throughout Scripture, chroniclers—inspired by the Spirit —recorded, encouraged, equipped, lamented, and presented the history, rules, redemption, and purpose of our King and this kingdom. Unfortunately, many of us today are living as followers of a King whom we also seek to dethrone, though perhaps not outrightly, through more subtle ways of complacency, autonomy, independence, or simply a lack of a connection to Him, His Word, writs, and covenants. As a result, we experience what anyone in any kingdom living apart from the rules of the King would—in our personal lives, homes, churches, communities, and our nation—the chaos that comes from rebellion.

In a kingdom, life is to be lived under the rule and authority of the King. The blessings of the covenantal charter of our

King in His Word, imbued with the authority He gives us through the Dominion Covenant along with His promises and His *chesed* love, come when we live all of our life under God. It comes when we live our lives on target with His kingdom agenda.

CHAPTER ONE

THE PURPOSE

If you are like me and you grew up in America, you were regularly reminded who you belonged to each time you said the pledge of allegiance or sang our national anthem in school or before sporting or civic events. It was clear our country did not want us to forget we are Americans. We recited the pledge day in and day out, allowing it to sink in, enabling each one of us to fully understand that no matter who we were, or what our background was—our history, gender, culture, or color—we belonged to this kingdom called the United States of America.

Even though the pledge had nothing directly to do with what was going on at that particular event or in the classroom, America wanted us to know it was only going on, and we were only able to participate in it, because we belonged to its kingdom.

In the same way our culture and our country wants us to be regularly reminded about our citizenship in this kingdom, there is another kingdom—a greater and more perfect kingdom—we are a part of. It is the kingdom of God.

Now, if you are an American, you are most likely an American because you were born here. If you are a part of the kingdom of God, it is because you have been born again into His kingdom. That's why you do not want to miss having a full comprehension of the kingdom: it not only affects you, it is also the key to understanding the Bible. The unifying central theme throughout the Bible is the glory of God and the advancement of His kingdom. The conjoining thread from Genesis to Revelation—from beginning to end—is focused on one thing: God's glory through advancing God's kingdom.

When you do not have that theme, then the Bible becomes disconnected stories that are great for inspiration but seem to be unrelated in purpose and direction. The Bible exists to share God's movement in history toward the establishment and expansion of His kingdom, highlighting the connectivity throughout which is the kingdom. Understanding that increases the relevancy of this several-thousand-year-old manuscript to your day-to-day living, because the kingdom is not only then, it is now.

The reason so many of us believers are struggling is we

want God to bless our agenda rather than us fulfilling His agenda. We want God to okay our plans rather than our fulfilling His plans. We want God to bring us glory rather than us bringing Him glory.

But it doesn't work that way. God has only one plan—His kingdom plan. We need to find out what that is so we can make sure we're working on God's plan—His agenda, not our own.

Throughout Scripture, God's agenda is His kingdom. The Greek word used for kingdom is *basileia*, which essentially means "rule" or "authority." A kingdom always includes three crucial components: first, a ruler empowered with sufficient authority; second, a realm of subjects who fall underneath this authority; and third, the rules of governance. God's kingdom is the authoritative execution of His comprehensive governance in all creation.

Therefore, the universe we live in is a theocracy. *Theos* refers to God. *Ocracy* refers to rule. A kingdom perspective means that the rule of God (theocracy) trumps the rule of man (homocracy). Psalm 103:19 (NIV) expresses it this way, "The LORD has established his throne in heaven, and his kingdom rules over all." The kingdom agenda is *the visible demonstration of the comprehensive rule of God over every area of life.*

God's kingdom is larger than the temporal, political, and social realms we live in. Nor is it confined to the walls of the church in which we worship Him. The kingdom is both now

(Mark 1:15) and not yet (Matthew 16:28). It is near us (Luke 17:21) but also in heaven (Matthew 7:21) since it originates from above, from another realm. Jesus revealed that truth shortly before His crucifixion when He said in response to Pilate, "My kingdom is not of this world. If My kingdom were of this world, then My servants would be fighting so that I would not be handed over to the Jews; but as it is, My kingdom is not of this realm" (John 18:36).

Since it originates from another realm, God established covenants within the world we live to implement it. These covenants are governmental systems or institutions designated as family, church, and civil government (state). God rules them all, and each one is to be accountable to Him and His standards as their sovereign. Whether or not mankind functions in alignment with His rule is another story.

Regardless, God has given the guidelines by which all three are to operate because He is the originator of all three. Failure to operate under His authority within those guidelines results in negative consequences. The three, while distinct in their responsibilities and jurisdiction, are to cooperate with each other with the common goal of producing personal responsibility and individuals who govern themselves under God. None of these governing spheres is to be viewed or is to operate as an all-powerful, centralized, and controlling authority over the others.

The foundation on which all three operate is an absolute

standard of truth. This standard of truth is nonnegotiable, non-adjustable, and transcends cultural, racial, and situational lines. Truth is fundamentally God-based knowledge since God is both the originator and the author of truth.

Not only does the kingdom agenda operate on this foundation of truth, but it also operates under the only all-inclusive principle presented to us for understanding the work of God and His kingdom. This principle is His glory. Romans 11:36 says, "For from Him and through Him and to Him are all things. To Him be the glory forever. Amen."

Glory simply means "to be heavy" or "to have weight." It denotes significance. Since all things come from God, are through God, and go to God, God's glory exists intrinsically in Himself. Whether we ascribe glory to God or not is irrelevant to the amount of glory God has; His glory is already fully present in Him. However, we experience and access that glory when we place ourselves under His comprehensive rule. This is because then God radiates and magnifies His glory to, in, and through us.

A primary position for bringing glory to God is surrender to His sovereignty. To surrender to God's sovereignty is to acknowledge His jurisdiction, along with the validity of His supremacy, over every area of life. God is accountable to no one. He either causes all things to happen, or He permits them to happen. Sovereignty means God never says: Oops, I missed that one. When we live by the principles of the kingdom agenda, we experience God's hand in every area of life and witness His promise to work all things together for good (Romans 8:28).

We often limit our opportunity to experience God working all things together for good by defining God according to our purpose rather than His. Humanism and socialism, whether it be in the form of modern-day church-ism, materialism, me-ism, statism, liberation theology, or Marxism, offer an insufficient understanding of the purpose, work, and revelation of God. It attempts to box God into a kingdom confined within the perspective of man. Yet when the human condition is used as the starting point for seeing the whole of God's revelation, rather than a surrender to His sovereignty over the whole of the human condition, faulty theology and sociology emerges. We wind up with a God fashioned in the image of man.

A kingdom perspective does not view man's condition first and assign to God what we feel would best reflect Him. Rather, a kingdom perspective ascertains how God has determined to glorify Himself and then aligns itself with that despite our inability to always understand God's processes. God *is* good, all the time. All the time, God is good. However, God's definition of good isn't always ours. In fact, God often uses the very thing we call "not good" as a tool to bring about an ultimate purpose, and the resultant manifestation of His greater glory.

For example, according to the covenant with Abraham in Genesis 15, slavery in Egypt was an intricate part of God's program for the nation. We read, "God said to Abram, 'Know for certain that your descendants will be strangers in a land that is not theirs, where they will be enslaved and oppressed four hundred years. But I will also judge the nation whom they will serve, and afterward they will come out with many possessions'" (Genesis 15:13–14).

The point here is that God, in accomplishing His kingdom agenda, allowed a negative reality that could have been avoided if He had chosen for it to be. Yet the reality of the Israelites' slavery in Egypt accomplished a higher purpose of establishing God's theocratic relationship with them. This relationship was based on an exodus that would serve as a constant reminder of who had brought them out (Exodus 12:41). This truth served as a foundational relational principle in the future movements of God with the Israelite community.

God's sovereignty in the midst of what we do not understand is echoed elsewhere throughout the Bible. Another example is found in the life of Joseph, who had been sold into slavery by his brothers. Joseph later said to his brothers, "As for you, you meant evil against me, but God meant it for good in order to bring about this present result, to preserve many people alive" (Genesis 50:20).

The freedom actualized through a kingdom perspective, that of embracing God's sovereignty, generates a faith more powerful than any human weapon or system of philosophy could ever produce. It accesses God's grace to grant a freedom not incumbent upon externals. This is the only true, authentic freedom as it manifests God's ability to bring about good in any and every situation surrendered to Him.

While God is a God of liberation and justice—and while we should be about the same—a kingdom perspective recognizes that in His sovereignty, His timing is not always the same as our own. However, a kingdom theology also recognizes that while oppression and injustice remain in the world's systems, they should never be tolerated within the church of God or among members within the body of Christ.

In fact, whenever Jesus proclaimed the kingdom of God during His earthly presence, He did so while simultaneously healing, helping, feeding, and freeing the hurting and the lost. Any church that minimizes legitimate social needs has failed to model itself after the One whom we have been given to follow, thereby reducing the glory it gives to God (Matthew 5:16).

While we may not always understand God's processes or His timing, a kingdom theology recognizes God's purpose does not change, and that purpose is to glorify Himself. The ultimate goal of the kingdom is always Godward. Therefore, living the kingdom agenda means the comprehensive rule of God is the final, authoritative, and governing principle in our personal lives, family lives, churches, and communities so God may manifest His glory while advancing His kingdom.

A LIFE OFF TARGET

King Edward III of England came to power in 1327 at the tender age of fourteen. He would prove himself to be, over his fifty-year reign, a focused and disciplined military leader. Under his charge, England rose from the laughingstock it had become under Edward's father to one of the fiercest, most formidable militaries in the world.

Not only did Edward require focus and discipline from himself, but he required it from those underneath him. He is known for having banned football and sports of any kind so people could direct their energies to practicing the art of the longbow. The longbow, new to the battle seasons of the English wars at Edward III's time, was the most sturdy piece of offensive weaponry in existence. Its draw weight alone was close to two hundred pounds. The arrows were three feet long and had tips that could tear through both chain mail and plate mail.

Victory would come with the longbow, of course, only when the arrows hit their targets. Ripping up doors, fences, or the like would do little to gain the upper hand in war. As such, warriors spent considerable time practicing the aim of their craft.

In this setting, imagine if you would, that there was a particular warrior who was aiming his bow toward the side of a barn. He was target shooting, practicing as his king—Edward III—had commanded. It was here he would shoot time and time again to hone his skill. When a passerby took a look at the side of the barn one day, he noticed that every single one of the arrows was smack-dab in the middle of the target. In fact, multiple arrows had all hit the target perfectly.

He asked the warrior, "How long did it take you to become so good at this?" To which the warrior replied, "Not long at all. In fact, it's simple."

Surprised at the frankness of his response, the passerby asked the warrior to show him how to do it. The warrior obliged and promptly shot twenty arrows, one right after another, at the side of the barn. The arrows landed anywhere and everywhere, but not within any target.

Then, without a second thought, the warrior walked over to the side of the barn and picked up some homemade paints and dye and started painting the targets around the arrows. He hadn't hit the targets at all. He had simply painted around his arrows.

I know what some of you may be saying: "Tony, kings and kingdoms are interesting, but I'm an American and we don't have kings anymore. None of this applies to me. And certainly not longbows." But give me a second to explain. Because even if you do not live in a visual, societal kingdom, if you are a follower of Jesus Christ, you belong to a kingdom. You belong to a King. Understanding what a kingdom is and how it runs is essential to living successfully as a part of the kingdom you are in now. And this story of the warrior with his painted targets, while fictitious, illustrates the situation our society is facing today.

Just like King Edward III could have never won the battles or restored order to his kingdom if he relied on warriors who simply painted targets around their arrows, God's kingdom and His agenda will fail to advance and have the impact it was designed to have on earth in history without the focus, discipline, and diligence of His subjects—which are us, today. Unfortunately, many of us do everything we can to give the impression our lives are on target when, in reality, all we have done is learn to paint well.

Not only are our nation, communities, churches, and families suffering as a result, but we are also suffering individually. Too many have sought to camouflage their emptiness and failure with materialism, the scramble for success and significance, and other pursuits. Some people even try to fill their emptiness through religious activities like church membership. They have learned how to look, talk, and act like Christians, but all of these things are simply "paint jobs" that try to obscure the fact we are a culture and a people tragically off target.

WHEN GOD *IS* THE PROBLEM

A quick glance at 2 Chronicles 15 reveals why we are so off target both spiritually and socially because it reveals three internal elements that plagued Israel, and which plague us today. I have taken the liberty of substituting America for Israel:

> And for many days *America* was without the true God and without a teaching priest and without law . . . In those times there was no peace to him who went out or to him who came in, for many disturbances afflicted all the inhabitants of *America*. And nation was crushed by nation, and city by city, for *God troubled them* with every kind of distress. (vv. 3, 5–6)

The nation faced an enormous decline because of its failure to recognize the one, true God, produce authentic teaching priests, and disciple their citizens in God's kingdom law.

In the situation of the Israelites, the first problem was that they wanted a convenient God, one they could control—a kingdom without a king. It was not that the majority had become atheists or snuffed out their sacrificial fires. Religion continued and rituals remained. It was that they had resorted to paying homage without alignment, reinforcing the culture's false view of a God who is harmless, distant, and has nothing significant to say about the educational, scientific, entertainment, racial, civic, political, familial, legal, or governing issues of the day.

The second problem the nation faced was a lack of teaching

priests. History doesn't record that there were no priests at all, just that the priests had stopped teaching the truth.

The issue of truth is all-important because a lack of truth leads to a "conscienceless" society. In the absence of truth, people lose their sense of right and wrong. Every person becomes a law unto himself, so chaos ensues.

The final problem in the nation was the lack of God's law. When a culture has a false view of God built on bad information, God begins to remove the restraint of His law, allowing evil to grow and spread unbridled. Even sinners who respect God's law won't do certain things. But once God's precepts are removed from or marginalized in a culture, the standard for a society is gone and the culture faces the consequences of turning against Him.

In Israel's chronicles, God was the cause of their distress, not the sinners in that culture, and not even Satan. It said, "God troubled them." In a situation like that, it doesn't matter who you elect or what programs you initiate. Until God's anger is assuaged, you will not be able to fix what is wrong or spend enough money to buy a way out of the dilemma.

As long as God is kept at a distance, He will not take over the control center of a nation, and unrighteousness will rule. He will be close enough for invocations and benedictions but not part of the decisions between.

The net result will be the devolution of mankind and a nation, as we are currently experiencing. The more we marginalize God and His kingdom agenda, the worse things will get. This is what Paul referred to when he wrote, "The wrath of God is revealed from heaven against all ungodliness and unrighteousness of men" (Romans 1:18). What America is witnessing today in the rapid deterioration of our culture is the reality that God is removing more and more of His restraint and revealing more and more of His wrath.

When God is the problem, only God is the solution.

TIME TO BRING ALL OF LIFE UNDER GOD

What must we do to reverse this downward spiral we are facing in our personal lives, families, churches, and communities? It is time to return to the King, His rules, and His agenda. What He says transcends human politics, secular social movements, and religious traditions.

It is time to recognize the kingdom of God is not some ethereal fairy tale located in some far-off land. It is both here and now. And just as some of the kings and queens of ages gone past poorly ruled the dominion given to them while others ruled well—it is up to each of us individually to write our own personal, and even family, legacy. And it is up to all of us collectively to write the legacy of our churches, community, and nation.

May it not be said of us, as it has been said of many kings and queens in the past, that this one—or that one—was simply unkingly. May it be said we accepted the responsibilities given to us as royalty and rulers under God to impact the realms He has given us for good, in His kingdom.

The Christian message, when communicated from a comprehensive, kingdom perspective, provides an agenda that can stand next to and above all other attempts to define the meaning of life, whether it be the individual, the family, the church, or the nation.

A kingdom agenda based on God's Word, rather than a secular agenda based on man's word, is the best way to make all of life work as our Creator intended.

Everyone has an idea and a viewpoint, but I believe God has spoken and He has not stuttered. There are two answers to every question: God's answer and everyone else's. And when they differ, everyone else is wrong. Thus it befits us to bring our lives under God's rule and passionately pursue His kingdom.

CHAPTER TWO

THE PERSON

As we start to go further on our journey through the depths, clefts, and mountaintops of God's kingdom, I want us to look at one fundamental truth. This truth is that God's kingdom originates from His realm, which is spiritual. The *origin* of God's kingdom is from above. It is not from the earth.

We see this in John 18:28–40, where Jesus appears before the Roman governor Pilate. The Jews want Jesus put to death, but they don't have the authority to carry out capital punishment. Since only Rome can do that, the Jews have to bring Jesus to Pilate to get his approval.

The Jews know exactly what accusation it will take to get Jesus executed by Rome. If He claims to be a king, He will be committing treason against Caesar (John 19:12). So they decide to make the charge against Jesus that He made Himself out to be a king.

If you call yourself a king, that implies you have a kingdom somewhere. So the first question Pilate asked Jesus was, "Are You the King of the Jews?" (John 18:33).

Notice Jesus' answer in verse 36: "My kingdom is not of this world. If My kingdom were of this world, then My servants would be fighting so that I might not be delivered up to the Jews; but as it is, My kingdom is not of this realm."

Now don't misread that. Jesus was not saying His kingdom is not *in* this world. He was saying His kingdom is not *of* this world. His kingdom does not originate from earth but from heaven. It is not derived from history but from the heavenlies. Jesus' servants weren't up in military arms about His arrest because He was not trying to overthrow the Roman militarily.

Jesus explained to Pilate, in my Evans' translation, "If My kingdom were of this world, My servants would be out there with their swords cutting off much more than just someone's ears. They would be going to war. If My kingdom were man-made, I would not be going to the cross without a battle."

Because Jesus represented another King from another kingdom that was not of this world, He did not resort to the methodologies of this world in order to defend or even advance it. The same holds true for you and me. To live your life according to the kingdom agenda will have an effect on your choices in life. Your decisions will not align with the world's wisdom or methods. A divine frame of reference will punctuate all you do.

Too many believers today are trying to find fulfillment and significance through human means. They are trying to discover their destinies through man's methods. However, man's methods never accomplish God's goals. Jesus revealed that fully when He answered Pilate straightforwardly. In essence, He said, "My method reflects My source." As believers, we are called to be in the world but not of the world. Similarly, a boat is made to be in the water but not of the water. If the boat begins to be of the water and starts taking on water, it will soon go down.

To be in the world and yet not of the world means the world or worldliness—that world order that seeks to leave God out—does not define your decisions, relationships, priorities, or even the cadence of how you flow. Your kingdom controls your methodology.

In verse 37 Jesus said something else significant. He said, "Everyone who is of the truth hears My voice." By this statement, Jesus assumed the existence of a body of truth. A kingdom agenda aligns itself with this body of truth. This reality places humanity in conflict with our culture, because we live in a world where a commitment to truth no longer exists. People want relative truth, not an absolute standard that says what is right and wrong, good and bad. Simply defined, truth is an absolute standard by which reality is measured. It is God's viewpoint on the matter.

If you are a follower of Jesus Christ you must believe in, accept, and align yourself according to the truth: that absolute, governing standard that transcends time, culture, ethnicity, gender, preference, and all else. This standard is comprised of the Word of God.

One of the major problems leading to the breakdown of society is we have far too many opinions dictating life choices and not enough truth mandating them. Even among Christians absolute truth isn't always the governing standard. We say things like, "Well, this is how I feel," or "This is what I think," or even "This is what my parents taught me."

While there is nothing necessarily wrong with thoughts or feelings, they shouldn't be the deciding factors to what is true. Truth transcends feelings. For example, you may feel like you have a headache so you take an aspirin. But the lab report might tell the truth that you have a brain tumor, and an aspirin won't do any good. Your head hurting felt real; it just didn't reveal the truth. When you miss the truth, you miss everything. Likewise, when you miss the truth of God's Word, you miss the kingdom.

Jesus was saying in John 18:37, "If you understand My kingdom, you would know the truth." The only lasting solutions to life are biblical solutions, because only biblical solutions are derived from a heavenly source and can address the cause-and-effect relationship between choices and consequences.

Here's what I mean by cause and effect when it comes to the kingdom. Everything visible and physical is always controlled or derived from what is invisible and spiritual. If you want to fix the visible and physical problems, you have to address the spiritual and invisible issues first.

Why? Because if you don't address the spiritual and invisible, you will not have addressed the divine precursor from which to solve the visible and physical issue at hand. What you can see, hear, touch, taste, and smell in your physical senses must first be addressed from God's perspective before you can make any lasting and real difference on the human level.

Satan wants to get us to skip the divine perspective, because he knows we will never be able to solve our visible and physical problems until we address them from the divine realm. Heaven rules earth. What happens up there determines what goes on down here. If you are not in contact with heaven, you shouldn't be surprised if you are in a quandary down here on earth.

God's kingdom agenda is much bigger than what we can see, hear, taste, or smell. It is also bigger than the political and social realms we function in. When you were saved, the kingdom of God was set up within you so it might be best positioned to reach outwardly while directing the circumference of your life.

Trusting Jesus Christ for your salvation will get you to heaven. But trusting Jesus Christ for your salvation doesn't automatically get heaven to come down to you. Getting into God's kingdom is through conversion, but getting God's kingdom operating in you is through commitment.

Commitment and dedication result only when the Jesus you placed your faith in is also the Jesus who rules within you—in the kingdom you are part of. God's kingdom goal is to manifest in history the operations of heaven. Therefore, when history is not reflecting heaven (Thy will be done, on earth as it is in heaven), God's kingdom is not visible. His kingdom is only visible in those areas and times when history emulates heaven.

WHO RULES?

Obviously at the heart of the kingdom is this concept of ruling. God told the first Adam to "Be fruitful and multiply, and fill the earth, and subdue it; and *rule* over the fish of the sea and over the birds of the sky and over every living thing that moves on the earth" (Genesis 1:28). God created mankind to rule. However, man gave up his rule when he was tricked by Satan. So God has extended this period of time called history for the proper reclaiming of the rulership that man has been given in God's kingdom on earth.

History is this process by which God is returning us to

the garden. In fact, history itself will end in the same place it began. The garden will be called the New Jerusalem—it is the place being prepared for those of us who believe in Jesus Christ as Lord and Savior when we die. We often call it heaven, but what many Christians do not grasp is that most of your time in the afterlife will be spent on earth, not in heaven. This is because God's purpose for humanity was earth.

We will be living in a new earth—with access to a new heaven. And all of this is made possible through the reclaiming of rulership made by the second Adam, Jesus Christ. When the first Adam failed to properly fulfill the dominion covenant to rule, Jesus Christ came—as the second Adam— to reinstate it.

When the first Adam rebelled against God, the Bible tells us that death fell upon all of us. Everyone who followed Adam inherited the curse of death. His destiny was imputed to us as the destiny of the human race because each of us is in Adam. Yet God gave a prophecy in the book of Genesis that would turn this thing around. We read in chapter 3 when God is talking about Satan, "And I will put enmity between you and the woman, and between your seed and her seed; He shall bruise you on the head, and you shall bruise him on the heel" (v. 15). Bear in mind that "head" refers to headship—rulership and authority. The seed of the woman will crush the headship of the serpent, or the devil. In other words, God was saying that someone who would be born of a woman would overcome the devil and reclaim authority and headship over the earth.

What is interesting to note in this verse, is how God chose to phrase it. Normally when talking about a seed—you would talk about the seed of a man. It is the male gender which carries the seed while the female gender carries the egg. God had determined to do a unique thing in producing a human being without the seed of a human man, but rather with the seed of a woman connected to His own divinity. Through this He would create the perfect God-Man, Jesus Christ, who would provide another plan, or opportunity, for regaining the rulership lost by the first Adam.

You can go through the entire Old Testament witnessing a back-and-forth scenario between Satan and the aim of this seed for rulership. A move toward the seed is created; then the counter-seed move is made by Satan. Once we reach the close of the Old Testament, we come into a four-hundred-year period of silence. This eventually ended through the onset of the New Testament where God begins by giving us the genealogy of the seed of Jesus Christ.

Up until this time, God would find a man and use a man to advance His kingdom on earth. Now God became a man in the person of Jesus Christ. Through a virgin birth He provided the opportunity for earth to become realigned properly again with Him and His Kingdom. In Jesus Christ, both heaven and earth were unified. The reason you see Pharaoh issuing a decree to kill all the newborn males in his land at the time of Moses' birth is the same reason you see Herod issuing a decree to kill every boy under the age of two at the time of Jesus Christ's birth. It is Satan, once again, working behind the scenes to get rid of the prophetic seed.

Because Satan's attempts failed, Jesus was able to live a sinless life, rise from the dead, ascend into heaven, and reclaim the Kingdom the first Adam had abandoned. Through the power of the cross and resurrection, Jesus Christ has ultimate authority in our world today. Satan no longer holds the final authority in believers' lives or on this earth.

POWER VERSUS AUTHORITY

God knows that and Satan knows that, but Satan doesn't want kingdom followers of Jesus Christ to know that. So he tries to intimidate, pressure, lie, etc., all to get kingdom followers to believe he still has power over them. The reason why so many people are not living lives reflective of the kingdom of God is they have lost sight of the reality that at the cross, Jesus Christ deactivated, dismantled, and disarmed Satan's headship. Jesus did this by stripping him of the ball Satan had recovered from the first Adam called "authority."

God has given the ultimate authority over what happens in history to His Son. He has placed all things in subjection to Him. As we read in Ephesians, "And He put all things in subjection under His feet, and gave Him as head over all things to the church, which is His body, the fullness of Him who fills all in all" (Ephesians 1:22–23).

One of the reasons we often don't live in light of this truth is because we confuse the terms "power" and "authority." Satan still has power. He still dominates the world we live in and influences people's lives in countless ways. He is as powerful now as he has ever been. His tactics and destruction are both real and damaging. But what he doesn't have is final authority. *Authority is the right to use the power that you possess.*

For example, on the football field the players are bigger and stronger—more powerful—than the referees. The referees are older, smaller, and more out of shape than the players. The players can knock you down—power. But the referees can put you out—authority. Satan has power, but the only way he is free to use that power over the lives of individuals, families, churches, or even the broader society is the failure to operate from under the rightful headship of the Lord Jesus Christ. Satan does not have the authority to use his power when men function under the covenantal covering of Jesus Christ.

This is why Satan will try so hard and long to lure people and divine institutions out from under the Lordship of Jesus Christ. He knows if he can get them out from under Christ's covering, he has free rein to deceive, trick, and harm them however he chooses. It is under the protective covering of the Lordship of Christ men stand protected.

Colossians 1:13 tells us God has "rescued us from the domain of darkness, and transferred us to the kingdom of His beloved Son." God rescued us from the authority of darkness and out of the wrong kingdom. By rescuing us, He transferred us to live our lives under the rule of a new King, Jesus Christ.

THE AUTHORITY OF THE WORD OF GOD

The supreme authority that an official holds on a football field by virtue of his office, the Bible holds by virtue of its Author, who is the King of creation and thus Ruler over all the earth. The Bible's authority is inherent in its every word and even every portion of a word, as we will see. The Bible is supremely authoritative because it is God's revelation in history. Just as there was no higher authority than the king, there is no higher authority you and I can appeal to than the Word of God.

The Bible's authority is timeless. For example, when we read in Exodus 20:3, "You shall have no other gods before Me," this command has the same force behind it today that it had when God first thundered these words to Moses more than three thousand years ago. This is important, because one problem I see as a pastor is that people disregard God's Word. To them, it's just ink on a page.

Our problem is we weren't there when God first spoke His Word—because if we had been there, we wouldn't be so casual about it. To get an idea of the terror that gripped Moses and all of Israel when God gave His commandments, read Hebrews 12:18–21. Even Moses said, "I'm so scared that I can barely even stand" (loosely translated).

The Bible is not simply words about God; it is the Word *of* God. Many people learn about God from the Bible, which is good—but that is not where you are to stop. The Word of God is the voice of God in print. It is active and alive and sharper than a two-edged sword, able to reach and instruct the deepest recesses and core of who you are (Hebrews 4:12).

Jesus was being challenged by His opponents one day when He tried to tell them that He was God. They objected, accused Him of blasphemy, and got ready to stone Him (see John 10:31–33). Jesus turned to the Scripture to make His case, and the way He used the Word has a lot to teach us about the Bible's authority.

"Jesus answered them, 'Has it not been written in your Law, "I said, you are gods"? If he called them gods, to whom the word of God came (and the Scripture cannot be broken), do you say of Him, whom the Father sanctified and sent into the world, "You are blaspheming," because I said, "I am the Son of God"?' " (vv. 34–36).

Jesus was using a powerful argument here. He said if the Bible—in this case the psalmist Asaph (Psalm 82:6)—used the term "gods" for men who were merely God's representatives, those who were accusing Jesus should not object if He called

ONE KINGDOM UNDER GOD

Himself God. Why? Because they had just seen Him heal a blind man (John 9) and do other miracles.

What I want you to see here is the binding authority of Scripture. Not even one word can be changed. Let me give you a term you may not have encountered before. Scripture is irrefragable, which means it cannot be voided or invalidated. How important is this trait? It was important enough to Jesus that He built a critical argument around it.

The Lord's opponents might have wished they could nullify or get around the word "gods" in Psalm 82:6, because it is the Hebrew word *Elohim*, which is one of the names of God. But Jesus had them, because God's Word called His representatives gods, and nothing could change the Scripture. Paul used a similar tactic in Galatians 3 to prove Jesus is Abraham's promised seed. The validity of Paul's entire point hung on the difference between the singular "seed" and the plural "seeds" (v. 16). Not only each letter of the Bible, but even the smallest part of each letter (see Matthew 5:18) is vital and carries God's authority.

In John 10:35–36 Jesus appealed to the authority and the inviolability of the Bible to argue that He was correct in saying, "I and the Father are one" (v. 30). His detractors understood clearly that Jesus was claiming to be God, and they wanted to stone Him for blasphemy (vv. 31–33). Jesus answered their charge by showing them that they could not reject Him without rejecting the Word of God they professed to believe.

That the Bible is completely authoritative and cannot be broken is a wonderful doctrine for the Christian faith. But the truth and power of God's Word can be nullified in your experience if you refuse to let the Word speak to you as it is or you start mixing it up with your human viewpoints.

Now please notice I did not say the Bible can lose its power or authority. That will never happen because God said His Word is "forever settled in heaven." (See Psalm 119:89.) But the Bible's power is blunted in our lives when we do not respond to God in humility and obedience.

This is probably the number one travesty people who claim to believe and follow God's Word commit against it. A lot of people who try to mix their own thoughts with the Bible's teaching have many degrees after their name. Education is fine, and the church has benefited from well-trained commentators and scholars who seek to understand what the Word means.

This is not what I'm talking about. There's a big difference between an honest attempt to understand the Bible as it reads and diluting its teachings with human thinking.

This thing of truth and authority is at the core of why the Holy Spirit is not doing more in our lives. The Spirit is the Spirit of Truth, who is obligated only to God's Word. When we start diluting the Word with our human viewpoints, the Spirit steps back because He is not going to bless our speculations. The introduction of human opinion nullifies the effectiveness of benefits the Scriptures are designed to give us.

Just before the closing benediction in Revelation, we find a dual warning to anyone who either "adds to" or "takes away from" the words of this book (Revelation 22:18–19). God pronounces a curse when people start messing with His message.

Biblical authority means God has the supreme right to determine our decision making and set the agenda for our lives. God doesn't want our rationalizations, but our response.

People can have Bibles in every room of the house, in their cars, and even at their offices, and yet still want to have their ears tickled by the latest religious fad or clever deceiver. God wants to occupy the place of supreme authority in your life, and He wants to set your life's agenda as you submit yourself to His Word.

Since Jesus possesses all authority, and His Word has all of His authority behind it, why are we as Christians not seeing God's Word at work any more than we are? I am convinced the reason is we are not living as though God's Word were our authority. We are not seeing more power in our lives and in the church at large because we aren't taking the Bible seriously.

THE DIVINE STANDARD

In every area of our lives, we must recognize that the authority we operate under goes far beyond our own human authority. God operates His Kingdom by His Word. The Bible is the authority and divine blueprint all of life is to be lived by. It is the benchmark by which all decisions should be made.

If you and I are going to advance God's Kingdom in history, we must recognize and submit to the divine authority of His Word. What was the first thing Satan got Adam and Eve to do in the garden? He got them to question the authority of God's Word. Satan specifically said, "Hath God *said* . . .?" Satan knew if he could get Adam and Eve to question, doubt, and ultimately change God's revealed Word to them, he could get them to disobey.

The Bible is not the Word of God emeritus. It is the manual of authority in God's Kingdom, the Book from which our Kingdom agenda is drawn. To the degree you honor, respect, and obey the Word, you will live the abundant life Christ came to give. To the degree you don't, you won't. You may have what appears to be a successful life to the outside world, but the abundant life is about so much more than outer appearances. It is the presence of peace coupled with the power of divine purpose.

The reason we need the Scripture as an authoritative document is found in Isaiah 55:8. God says, "My thoughts are not your thoughts, nor are your ways My ways." God doesn't act the way we act. He doesn't think like we think. He functions in a totally different sphere that we call His transcendence. He is totally distinct from and above His creation.

If God did not reveal His will and His standard to us, we could never figure it out on our own. Often in the Bible God makes the statement "I am not a man" (see Numbers 23:19). The idea is, "Then don't measure Me by your standards, because you and I are not alike."

Since God is the only true authority in His Kingdom, we must live under His revealed authority. If you had a messed-up life and said, "Tony, help me with my messed-up life," I would open the Bible and show you God's standard for fixing a messed-up life.

If you came to me with a messed-up family and said, "Tony, help me with my messed-up family," I would open up the same Book and show you how the Author of the family determined the family should be run.

The same thing is true for a messed-up church. The Bible is the charter of the church, and only the Bible can fix a messed-up church.

And if the governor or the president came to me and said, "Evans, we have a messed-up state" or "a messed-up country," I wouldn't switch books. I would open up the Bible and offer the governor or the president God's solution for a broken-down society.

Even in a democracy there must be a transcendental ethical norm serving as the standard for making laws so a legitimate democracy can work. Without a standard, democracy has no anchor to hold the majority in check, lest the will of a majority lead to unrestrained national government or the uncontrolled evil desires of that majority. The Bible provides the standard.

Why would I use the same Book in all four situations? Because all four areas of kingdom life—personal, family, church, and civil government—are created by God and governed by His Word.

There are Christians who want to switch books. They want to use the Bible when it's convenient, like making God a servant in His own kingdom. But it won't work. The Bible must be the authority that governs every area of life.

Since the Bible is God's rule book for life in His kingdom, let's consider how the authority of the Bible impacts the four areas of God's kingdom mentioned above. Remember as we go that no one is supreme and sovereign but God, so He has the right to draw up the rules of kingdom life. The Word of God reveals the absolute standard to which all other standards must bow, since it is right about everything it speaks on, and it speaks about everything.

We must take seriously the whole Bible, including the revelatory aspects of the Old Testament. Paul told Timothy, who did not yet have a New Testament to read, that the Scripture (Old Testament) was sufficient for all of life (see 2 Timothy 3:16–17).

The statements of particular Old Testament regulations may differ in their contemporary application. But the clear principles of Old Testament truth as they reflect the character of God and the operation of His kingdom apply to us since "they were written for our instruction" (1 Corinthians 10:11). Since the typological nature of the old covenant is true of the new covenant, providing us wisdom for all of life today. Furthermore, Israel is the only government legislated by God, thus it is the only place we can look to for guidance on how government should work and reflect the character of God. This is the effect Israel's government was to have on other nations: to serve as a paradigm for them to emulate (see Deuteronomy 4:5–8).

THE "TEN WORDS"

Jesus said it best when He said in Matthew 4:4, "Man shall not live on bread alone, but on every word that proceeds out of the mouth of God." Life itself is tied to biblical authority. If you rebel against it, you're rebelling against life.

Moses told Israel, "All the commandments that I am commanding you today you shall be careful to do, that you may live" (Deuteronomy 8:1). Life and death in God's kingdom are tied to the issue of biblical authority. We need to know God's commandments so we can do them and live.

You may be saying, "Tony, the Bible is a big book. It's got sixty-six smaller books inside. It takes a lifetime to understand the Bible. How can I possibly do it?"

Let me suggest the Bible is not quite as hard as you may

think. Yes, it's so inexhaustible that theologians take a lifetime to try to understand it. Yet God's Word is so clear children can grasp it.

The Bible has relatively few core teachings. Now it may talk about them in a thousand different ways, but the Bible only has a handful of foundational truths. Let me show you what I mean.

Exodus 20 contains what Moses called literally the "ten words." We know them as the Ten Commandments. They are the summary of life, the foundation and essence of God's law. Now God added about 613 stipulations to break out the commandments in more detail. But these "ten words" summarize what God expects.

If you understand the Ten Commandments you will have the core of what God expects from His kingdom subjects.

Even better, Jesus summarized the essence of these commandments for us in Matthew 22:36–40. A lawyer came to Jesus and asked Him a lawyer-type question: "Which is the greatest commandment in the Law?"

Jesus told him, "You shall love the Lord your God with all your heart, and with all your soul, and with all your mind . . . The second [commandment] is like it, 'You shall love your neighbor as yourself'" (vv. 37, 39).

There you have the very core of God's kingdom agenda. You don't have to go to seminary to know the two most important things God would have you do on earth are to love

Him with all of your heart, soul, and mind, and to love others as you love yourself. Understanding these principles governs your personal life. In the words of Solomon, "Fear God and keep His commandments, because this applies to every person" (Ecclesiastes 12:13).

Since God's Word is the authority in our personal lives, and since He has specific instructions for us to keep, where do we get the motivation to keep His Word? To the unrighteous it will be fear of judgment.

The motivation for the righteous is appreciation for God's grace. You and I keep God's Word out of gratitude because we recognize it's by His grace we are even here. All the motivation Israel needed to keep the Ten Commandments was provided back in Exodus 20:2, before the commands were given: "I am the LORD your God, who brought you out of the land of Egypt, out of the house of slavery."

If you know the Lord Jesus Christ as your Savior, He has set you free. Duty ought to rise out of devotion. He shouldn't be begging you to keep His commandments. Not only that, the motivation comes in knowing God only backs His own Book. If you want God's authority and power to override your circumstances rather than continually being under your circumstances, start aligning your personal life according to His Word.

CHAPTER THREE

THE PRESENCE

Believers used to belong to Satan's kingdom and rulership before meeting Christ, but now Christians are part of a new kingdom where Jesus Christ is the King. Satan, in order to rule the lives and institutions of kingdom followers, needs to get them to leave the kingdom rule of Jesus Christ and come back over to his.

Much of this happens through the division of the secular and the sacred. This is done when people attend and participate in church under one kingdom. Then they go out into the world Monday through Saturday and function there under the influence of another kingdom. There are studies done of the Bible in one kingdom. Then there is socializing done with friends in another kingdom. Essentially we witness this flip-flop of kingdoms and wonder why there is not more victory and rule in lives, homes, churches, and communities.

The answer is simple: Satan is ruling people's lives because they are yielding the power to him—not by way of any rightful authority that he has, but simply because of a failure to align their thoughts and decisions under the King of the kingdom. Through abandoning the union we were created to have with Christ under His headship, authority is lost. By not giving Jesus Christ the proper place in our hearts, homes, churches, and our world—the first place He deserves—we lose His covering. All of life for a kingdom follower should be summed up in the recognition of the Lordship of Jesus Christ.

> He is the image of the invisible God, the firstborn of all creation. For by Him all things were created, both in the heavens and on earth, visible and invisible, whether thrones or dominions or rulers or authorities—all things have been created through Him and for Him. He is before all things, and in Him all things hold together. He is also head of the body, the church; and He is the beginning, the firstborn from the dead, so that He Himself will come to have first place in everything. (Colossians 1:15–18)

With the resurrection and exaltation of Jesus Christ, He has been made head over all rulers and authority. He is in charge. When a person accepts Jesus Christ as their sin-bearer, they have transferred kingdoms. Jesus Christ is to be preeminent in their life—He is to have first place in all things. Only as the Lordship and Kingship of Christ is acknowledged and submitted to can the power and authority of God's kingdom be made visible in history. God explicitly states it is His intentional purpose to bring all of history under the rule of Jesus Christ (Ephesians 1:9–10).

Transferring kingdoms can best be illustrated by what happens when a single woman gets married. When she marries, she is transferred from the kingdom of her father to the kingdom of her husband. She is no longer underneath her father's headship, but under her husband's headship. The surest way to have problems in a family is for a married woman to go to her father to overrule her husband in her life choices. When that happens there is inevitably a conflict of kingdoms.

As children of God, we have been transferred from the kingdom of darkness into the kingdom of Jesus Christ. Problems arise when we start listening to the old head, Satan, who owns and runs the kingdom of darkness. This brings us in direct conflict with the kingdom of God.

The second chapter of Colossians gives us an insightful look into the explosive and powerful nature of our union with Christ when we are aligned properly under His kingdom rule. We read,

See to it that no one takes you captive through hollow and deceptive philosophy, which depends on human tradition and the basic principles of this world rather than on Christ. For in Christ all the fullness of the Deity lives in bodily form, and you have been given fullness in Christ, *who is the head over every power and authority*. And in Him you were also circumcised with a circumcision made without hands, in the removal of the body of the flesh by the circumcision of Christ, having been buried with Him in baptism, in which you were also raised up with Him through faith in the working of God, who raised Him from the dead. (See Colossians 2:8–12.)

Likewise, we read in Ephesians,

Even when we were dead in our transgressions, (God) made us alive *together* with Christ (by grace you have been saved), and raised us up *with* Him, and seated us *with* Him in the heavenly places *in* Christ Jesus. (Ephesians 2:5, 6, italics added)

To apply this truth to individual lives, if you are a believer in Jesus Christ, when Christ died, you died with Him. When Christ arose, you arose with Him. When Christ was seated at the right hand of the Father, you were seated with Him.

In other words, you were made to function in concert and cadence with Jesus Christ.

In order for you to legitimately access His sovereign authority over all things, you and your world must be aligned underneath His headship. This includes your thoughts, choices, words, and perspective. In properly aligning yourself under Him and His Word, His authority becomes manifest in your own life as you seek to advance God's kingdom on earth.

An individual can go to all the church services they want, read all the spiritual books they want—in fact, they can name and claim whatever they want—but until they place themselves under the comprehensive rule of God in every area of their life by aligning themselves under the Lordship of Jesus Christ, they will not fully realize nor maximize the rule and authority He has destined for them.

God has appointed a regent—Jesus Christ, who has been elevated above all—to rule over history. Believing in God is not enough to access the authority that comes through Christ. Calling on God's name is not enough. The relationship with Jesus Christ determines what happens in history because He has been placed above all rule and authority and, by virtue of who He is, demands first place. Because Jesus is seated at the right hand of God (the power side of God), His followers are seated there with Him (Ephesians 2:6).

I know what you are saying: "But, Tony, how can someone

be in two places at one time?" Easy; we do it all the time through technology. I can physically be in Dallas, but I can also be on Skype in Chicago. I can be seated in my home in Dallas and participate in a board meeting in Atlanta. Through human technology we can be in two places at one time.

If man can produce technology that can put us in two places at one time, don't you think the Creator of the universe can do the same thing? You are physically on earth, but you are supposed to be functioning from the position of heaven. You are seated with Christ in the heavenlies. What the enemy does is try to keep you physically on earth and operating physically on earth.

If he can keep believers thinking we are here—bound by the rules of his kingdom rather than accessing the authority of Jesus Christ in the heavenlies, he can keep us perpetually defeated and keep our world broken. The only authority that is the final authority is the authority that comes from Christ. Each of us must operate from a divine point of view rather than a human point of view.

Have you ever been watching cable television only to have the channel go out and the words "searching for signal" come on your screen? That's what has happened to many believers who do not live their lives under the Kingship of Jesus Christ. They are cut off from accessing His rightful authority. It's not that they don't have the ability to access His authority; they have an interruption in the signal. The enemy has been allowed to somehow interfere with the communication and alignment they have with Jesus Christ.

ALIGNING THROUGH CONFESSING

The word "confess" means to openly and publicly affirm and declare where a person stands on an issue. Part of alignment under the authority of Jesus Christ involves a willingness to publicly declare and demonstrate commitment to and an association with Him. To put it another way, if you are a secret-agent Christian or a spiritual CIA representative, you have not made Jesus Lord in your life. We read in the kingdom book of Matthew,

> "Therefore everyone who confesses Me before men, I will also confess him before My Father who is in heaven. But whoever denies Me before men, I will also deny him before My Father who is in heaven." (Matthew 10:32, 33)

Based on this verse, the question stands: If you were accused of being a Christian on your job, would there be enough evidence to convict you, or would you be found innocent of all charges? Jesus makes a clear tie between His followers' public acknowledgment and confession of Him before men and His confession of us before the Father. Keep in mind,

Jesus doesn't say if you confess My Father before men, I will confess you before Him. It's easy to say you believe in God. People pour so many variant definitions into the one word "God" that just saying "God" doesn't mean much anymore. However, when you publicly confess Jesus Christ, everyone knows who you are talking about. The name *Jesus* is ultra specific.

Confessing Jesus publicly can be compared in some degree to a married person wearing a wedding ring. That wedding ring is there on the ring finger to make a public declaration that there is a legal and binding relationship with someone else. You can be married and choose not to wear your ring so no one will know you are married, but I doubt your spouse will smile on that choice.

There are a lot of Christians today who have married into the family of God as the bride of Jesus Christ who don't want to wear His ring. They don't want other people to know they are bound to Jesus in a covenantal relationship. Like Peter, when it is not convenient for them to be associated with Jesus, they simply say, "I don't know the man." However, because of this choice, Jesus makes it clear that when they are calling on Him and He is acting as Mediator between them and God the Father, He will also deny He knows them. As long as a Christian is a secret agent saint, he or she won't be accessing or maximizing both the kingdom power and authority rightfully his or hers through the Lordship of Jesus Christ.

Jesus declares that a person's willingness to confess Him becomes the marker of their seriousness about Him. It is much more than simply believing in God. In fact, Satan believes in God. Alignment under the Kingship of Christ—putting Him in first place—involves publicly declaring and demonstrating an association with Him in both words and actions.

When my son Jonathan, who now serves as chaplain to the Dallas Cowboys, played football, he was a fullback. The job of a fullback is to run interference for a halfback. The halfback gets the ball while the fullback goes out in front of him, because there is an enemy trying to tackle the halfback. The fullback's mission is to get rid of the enemy so the halfback can get through the line.

Jesus' full-time job as Lord and Savior is to run interference for each of us as His kingdom followers. Satan, our enemy, is seeking to defeat us. He is seeking to overwhelm us. What we need to keep in mind is that we have a blocker out in front.

However, Jesus has stated clearly He's not going to block for any of us if we won't acknowledge or confess Him. Why should He run interference for someone who is just going to deny that He is there? I'm sure you don't like the feeling that comes when someone has used you. When they have taken advantage of what you have to offer—whether in your home, in a relationship, at the church, or even at your work. They have reaped the benefits from you, but they give you none of the rewards or the credit. It is as if you weren't a part of the successes they are enjoying, even though you were an integral part of it.

The next time this situation arises where you are called upon to help this person out, your motivation to do it well may be a lot less than before. This is simply because no one likes the feeling of being used. We are relational beings, and we appreciate being acknowledged in our relationships.

Jesus is no different. Why should He transform our lives and our world only to be forgotten or overlooked? He states clearly: Confess Me before others, and I've got your back. Marginalize, sideline, or dismiss Me . . . and you've got your own back. The question on the floor for Christians today is who do you want to have your back? You or Jesus?

CONFESS AND BELIEVE

In the book of Romans, Paul writes a great document on theology to the Christian church. But in chapter ten, he comes to two verses that have confused a lot of people over the years. They read,

> That if you *confess* with your mouth Jesus as Lord, and *believe* in your heart that God raised Him from the dead, you will be saved; for with the heart a person

believes, resulting in righteousness, and with the mouth he confesses, resulting in salvation." (Romans 10:9, 10, italics added)

In these two verses we read two things we must do to be *saved*: confess with our mouth and believe in our heart. The problem comes because every other place in the New Testament that tells us how to get saved tells us we only have to do one thing: believe (John 3:16, Acts 16:31, John 5:24, Romans 4:4, 5). Yet in the book of Romans, we have to do a second thing. So either the Bible is contradicting itself, or this passage in Romans must mean something else.

The answer to that dilemma comes in the context of the passage. Paul is not instructing sinners on how to become saints in this passage. He is instructing saints on how to get delivered (saved). You must believe on the Lord Jesus Christ to go to heaven, but you must confess the Lord Jesus Christ to get heaven to come to you.

Let me explain. When a person accepts Jesus Christ as their personal Savior (believe), His righteousness is immediately imputed to them as their righteousness. They are saved, in the eternal sense of the word. Yet when they make a public confession of Jesus Christ as their Lord, they receive His deliverance in the here and now, in history.

The word "saved" means to be rescued, or delivered. The reason why a lot of people who are going to heaven are not seeing heaven join them in history is because they have believed but they have not confessed. In other words, they have declared within themselves whom they are trusting for their salvation. They have placed their faith in Jesus Christ for the forgiveness of their sins. But they have not made an ongoing public confession, or declaration, of Him as their Lord—whether through word or deed.

In biblical days in Rome, Christians would be brought before the magistrates because they were declaring Jesus as Lord in both speech and actions. The term "Lord" means supreme ruler or authority. The Roman authorities would attempt to get the Christians to declare Caesar as Lord and deny Jesus as supreme ruler and authority. Believing in Jesus didn't get the Christians hung or tossed to the lions for sport. Believing in Jesus as the rightful ruler and Lord did. There's a difference.

Frequently throughout the New Testament the disciples and the apostles regularly referred to themselves as slaves. Even the book of Romans opens up with these words, "Paul, a bond-servant of Christ Jesus . . . " (Romans 1:1). A bond servant is translated from *doulos* which literally means "slave." A slave is someone who has a master or a lord. Declaring Jesus as your Savior takes you to heaven, but declaring Jesus as your Master, or Lord, brings heaven to you. In acknowledging your rightful place under Jesus as His *doulos*, or slave, you get His delivering power on earth.

The reason why we may not be seeing more of God's

rescue and deliverance in individual lives, homes, churches, and communities is because we have Jesus positioned as our Savior, but not as our Lord. We, the collective body of Christ, are not His slaves. Keep in mind the job of a slave is do whatever the Master says to do. It's as straightforward as that.

Unfortunately, today Jesus has too many other masters in most of our lives He has to compete with. The important thing to remember is Jesus is not willing to be one among many. He is not willing to be part of an association or club. Neither is He willing to be relegated to being a personal assistant. Jesus as Lord means Jesus is to be *the* supreme ruler and master. He calls the shots, and He is to be acknowledged in everything that is done. The problem is too many people want a Savior but don't want a Lord. Because of this, a number of individuals today are experiencing the result of denying Christ publicly. They are likewise being denied by Christ before God the Father.

How does this denial occur? Several other passages in both the Old and New Testament will give us insight. Let's read them first:

> For "whoever will call on the name of the Lord will be saved." (Romans 10:13)

> Paul, called as an apostle of Jesus Christ by the will of God, and Sosthenes our brother, To the church of God

which is at Corinth, to those who have been sanctified in Christ Jesus, saints by calling, with all who in every place call on the name of our Lord Jesus Christ, their Lord and ours. (1 Corinthians 1:1, 2)

And it will come about that whoever calls on the name of the LORD will be delivered. (Joel 2:32)

These are just a few passages, but we can see clearly that those being addressed are already saved from an eternal standpoint. They are "saints by calling." The word "deliverance" doesn't mean salvation in view of eternity. In the context of these passages and the passage we read earlier in Romans 10, deliverance is God's help in history. Calling on the name of the Lord invokes heaven to join you down here.

Let me explain how this works. Let's say I was to call on God to deliver me from something I was struggling with or a circumstance I was facing. It was too much for me to bear or overcome on my own, and I needed to be delivered. So I call on the name of the Lord. When that happens, God the Father, turns to Christ the Son, and says, "Son, Tony Evans just called on Me because he wants to be rescued from a particular situation. What do you say?"

Jesus responds, "Father, Tony Evans never wants to bring up My name in public. He's embarrassed about his association with Me. He does not want Me to influence his decision making. Whenever religion comes up, he changes the subject. He'll use Your name—God, but he won't ever mention mine—Jesus Christ. He's never willing to share his faith with anyone. If You answer his request for deliverance, all You are doing is giving him a new opportunity to deny Me. Based on that, I would recommend You deny his request since he denies Me."

Hopefully none of that is true in the literal sense relating to me since I've made it my life mission to declare Jesus Christ publicly. But you get the point. You can call on the name of the Lord all you want for deliverance, but according to Romans 10:9–10, if you have not also confessed the name of the Lord you call on, your request could be denied. To experience heaven's authority and power on earth, a person must be willing to confess Jesus Christ as Lord publicly in what they say and do.

You believe on Him for eternal salvation. You confess Him publicly for deliverance in history. Both His investment and His involvement in your life hinges upon your public declaration through both words and actions that He is Lord. Paul told Timothy boldly, "Therefore do not be ashamed of the testimony of our Lord" (2 Timothy 1:8).

If for no other practical reason than accessing the power of deliverance on earth, you must establish and declare Jesus Christ as Lord in your life and over your world. You must open your mouth publicly and let others know through what you say and through what you do that He is your Lord and Master—that you are not ashamed to be associated with Him. He is seated at the right hand of God in the heavenlies, as are you through His redemption on the cross. Access His power and authority through a public declaration of His Lordship in your life. His blood has established the New Covenant under which you are to align your life and world in order to receive its full covenantal covering and protection (Romans 12:11).

You've probably heard someone say, "I plead the blood." They are talking about the blood of the covenant. However, the way you plead the blood of the covenant is not simply by saying some magical words. You plead the blood of the covenant by being under the terms of the covenant—by making Jesus Christ Lord of your life and ruler of your world.

In the Old Testament times, the Israelites couldn't just say, "I plead the blood." No, they had to put the blood on the doorposts in order to plead it. It involved more than merely saying it. They had to align themselves within the protective confines of the walls that were connected to the blood-stained doors. Likewise, today there must be covenantal alignment under the Lordship and rulership of Jesus Christ in order to experience His kingdom power, authority, provision, and covering.

We read about this New Covenant in the book of Hebrews where it says,

> But now He has obtained a more excellent minis-
> try, by as much as He is also the mediator of a *better
> covenant*, which has been enacted on better promises.
> (Hebrews 8:6, italics added)

For this reason He is the mediator of a *new covenant*, so
that, since a death has taken place for the redemption of the
transgressions that were committed under the first covenant,
those who have been called may receive the promise of the
eternal inheritance. (Hebrews 9:15, italics added)

> And to Jesus, the mediator of a *new covenant*, and
> to the sprinkled blood, which speaks better than the
> blood of Abel. (Hebrews 12:24, italics added)

Jesus Christ is the Lord of the new covenant, the unique,
one-of-a-kind mediator between heaven and earth (1 Timothy 2:5).

Friend, I have a master key to the church where I pastor.
My key can work in any lock. A person who works at the
church may have a key to their own office, or even to the
section of the building their office is in. But they are limited
in which doors they can open.

Because I have a master key, I can go anywhere in the
church I want to go.

A lot of us are not getting everywhere we need to go

because we don't have the Master key. We've got keys for certain rooms. We come to church, hear a sermon, and receive a truth so we have a key for a certain room in our Christian lives. We must understand, however, the key to the Christian life for the church of Jesus Christ—for our homes and our communities—is Jesus Christ as King and Master. The ability to live victoriously and advance God's kingdom agenda on earth comes through this unique Master key called the Kingship of Christ.

Only as the Kingship of Jesus Christ is reflected through His people individually and corporately will the world experience the rule of God as the Creator intended it to be.

CHAPTER FOUR

THE PEOPLE

If you, like me, are a citizen of the United States of America, you fall underneath a covenantal document called the Constitution. The Constitution is the umbrella document that covers the operations of the kingdom called the USA. This particular constitution is unique from many historical documents in that it declares much by a proclamation of freedom.

You may hear people regularly say if they feel that they have been treated unjustly, "I know my rights," and then they will appeal to their constitutional rights within the kingdom called America—in particular to the amendments attached to the Constitution.

If you are a Christian, you are also part of another kingdom as we have been discussing—the kingdom of God. As such, you also have covenantal rights, privileges, and authority. Yet if you do not know those rights, or how to properly exercise your rights, you can be illegitimately oppressed simply because you are not operating by the instructions or functioning under the umbrella of God's kingdom covenant. Covenants are the mechanism by which God administers His kingdom.

Before moving on, let me first define a covenant. In the Bible, a covenant is a divinely created bond. It is a *spiritually binding relationship between God and His people inclusive of certain agreements, conditions, benefits, responsibilities, and effects.* God's power, provisions, and authority to His people operate under His covenants.

Whenever God wanted to formalize His relationship with His people, He would establish a covenant. There are a number of these agreements in Scripture such as the Abrahamic Covenant, the Mosaic Covenant, the Davidic Covenant, and the New Covenant.

A covenant involves far more than a contract. In a biblical covenant, you not only sign on the dotted line but you enter into an intimate relationship with the other person or persons in the covenant.

In other words, covenants are predicated on a relationship. That's not necessarily true in a contract. You can sign a contract to buy a home and have no personal relationship at all with the seller. You may not even know or like the seller. Likewise you can sign a business deal because the deal makes sense but have no affiliation or relationship with the other party beyond the deal itself.

It is not so in a covenant. One of the primary components that distinguishes a covenant is the reality that it is entered into as a relational agreement. Marriage, for example, is a covenant and not solely a contract. Marriage not only includes a binding agreement, but it also binds the people involved in an intimate relational union.

A covenant is also a relationship of blessing. Whenever God makes a covenant, His intent is for the good of those who covenant with Him. When you enter into a covenant with God, it is so that "you may prosper in all that you do" (Deuteronomy 29:9).

God takes His covenants very seriously, as they are the mechanism by which His kingdom functions. Because of this, covenants are inaugurated in Scripture through a specific process, including an element of blood. In fact, often covenants were signed, or ratified, in blood. God's covenants are so serious, significant, and meaningful that they are inaugurated by nothing less than the essence which sustains life itself.

Take marriage as an example again. When a husband and wife come together on the first night, if the wife is a virgin she may bleed. Now that is not just a physiological reality, but a theological reality. The woman's blood signifies the inauguration of the covenant.

God's covenants are serious and inaugurated by blood because they are meant to make a statement about a significant relationship that has been instated under His rule. You and I are part of God's kingdom, and we are there by a covenant sealed with nothing less than the blood of Jesus Christ Himself.

The question may arise as you are reading this chapter, "Why do I need to understand the covenant in order to understand the kingdom?" The answer is simple: Because God's provisions, promises, and even His preferred will flows through His covenant. If you do not know and operate under the covenant, you cannot exercise the authority you legally possess.

One of the reasons the devil is winning so much in spiritual warfare is because God's followers are not functioning in concert with the covenant and are not benefitting from the authority of the kingdom.

In Exodus chapter 19 we see an interesting statement about a covenant. We read God speaking these words,

> Now then, if you will indeed obey My voice and keep My covenant, then you shall be My own possession among all the peoples, for all the earth is Mine; and you shall be to Me a kingdom of priests and a holy nation. (v. 5–6a)

In this passage we hear God telling Moses that if the Israelites will keep His covenant, they will be a special (holy) people uniquely separated for His purposes. They will not simply be another person or group of people. They will be set apart for God's use in a special way. The word "holy" means "set apart, unique."

As a believer functioning under the umbrella of God's covenant, you are positioning yourself to be set apart for God's kingdom purposes as well. God's covenant is specifically tied to His relationship with you in how He works both in and through you to advance His kingdom on earth.

Another passage that affords us insight into the function of a covenant is found in the book of Deuteronomy. Chapter 29 of this book opens up with a specific reference to a covenant God is making. It says, "These are the words of the covenant which the LORD commanded Moses to make with the sons of Israel in the land of Moab, besides the covenant which He had made with them at Horeb" (v. 1). Next the passage goes into the details of the covenant. What is of particular interest to our examination of covenants in this chapter is written in verse 9. Read these words closely: "So keep the words of this covenant to do them, *that you may prosper in all that you do*" (italics added).

Let me tell you a secret about God's covenants: They are designed to benefit you. Keeping the terms of the covenant allows you to "prosper in all that you do." Covenants produce progress in your life. Progression is clearly tied to covenant keeping. Only as you operate in and under the covenant do you receive the flow of God's power, position, provision, and authority. Covenantal positioning is key to partaking of kingdom privileges.

A synonym for covenant is *covering*. If and when you operate under God's covenant, you are operating under His covering. Look at it like this: When it is raining outside and the thunder and lightning fill the sky, you most likely reach for your umbrella before heading out into the rain. You will open up your umbrella and place it over your head. Now you are covered.

The umbrella does not stop the sky from raining, but it does stop the rain from reaching you. While it does not change what is happening around you, it does change what happens to you. Similarly, when you are under God's covering in His covenant, the circumstances, trials, and challenges of life may not change but God will cover you so they do not negatively impact you as they would without His covering. To be under His covenant is to experience the protection of His covering.

What is interesting about the covering of the covenant is that it is a lot like the armor of God Paul speaks about in Ephesians 6. The armor is there to protect you, but if you do not "put on" the armor, it does you little good. Likewise, if you have an umbrella and it is raining yet you leave the opened umbrella in another location rather than hold it over you—or have it and refuse to open it—the umbrella will not fulfill its function. You will still get rained on. In order to fully benefit from God's covering—His power, provisions, and authority—you not only must be *in* His covenant, but you must align yourself *under* His covenantal rule in your life.

You can be a Christian all day long, but if you are not aligned according to the conditions and rules of the covenant, you will lack the full covering and provision of the kingdom. Just like in America you may lose some of your rights to freedom if you break the laws that govern the nation, covenantal covering comes tied to the aspects of God's covenant. If you desire to live your life full of kingdom authority, power, protection, and provision, covenantal positioning is key.

THE FACETS OF A COVENANT

To complete our look at covenants, I want to explore the facets of the covenant. These are the five distinctives that make up a spiritual covenant and must be recognized for you to be in covenantal alignment. These include transcendence, hierarchy, ethics, sanctions, and inheritance.

TRANSCENDENCE

The first facet of a covenant is a theological word called *transcendence*. Transcendence simply means God is in charge. We call this attribute of God His sovereignty. Transcendence also references God as distinct. He is not a part of His creation, but rather separate from it, above it. Therefore, covenants are both initiated and ruled by God.

That might seem like an obvious statement and one we don't need to spend too much time on, but transcendence is a key principle in a covenant. In order for a covenant to successfully function, carrying with it both the benefits and security a covenant supplies, it has to be set up according to God's expectations and regulations.

Covenants can never operate without the ongoing involvement of God. Biblical, spiritual, and theological covenants assume God's integration into every aspect of the covenantal relationship in order for that covenant to work.

When the practical realities of God are dismissed from any covenantal relationship, it becomes an invitation to the devil to create havoc in the realm. This happens because there has been a departure from transcendence.

If you are going to come under God's rules, if you are going to serve in God's government, if you are going to be blessed as part of God's Kingdom, you cannot neglect the reality that God is in charge. Sometimes at work the boss has to remind people who is in charge. The same is true with God. Often He has to remind His followers who is in charge, and He does this through myriad ways.

Look at King Nebuchadnezzar of Babylon as one example.

Nebuchadnezzar looked out over his balcony one day and said, "Look at this great Babylon *I have built*. I'm in charge here."

You may know the story in Daniel 4:28–37. As a result of Nebuchadnezzar's pride, God allowed his mental health to dip into madness. His nails began to grow, his hair became wild, and for seven years he lived like a beast in the field. But then he came back to his senses and stood on his balcony one more time. Only this time Nebuchadnezzar said, "Let everybody in Babylon know *God is in charge*."

The question you must raise about being under God's covenant and in God's Kingdom is this: Is He in charge? Or are you trying to live independently of His "in-chargeness"? If you are, you are in rebellion against His covenant.

You are either a friend or an enemy of the King based on whether you pray "Thy will be done" or "My will be done." Transcendence means God is in charge.

HIERARCHY

A second facet of God's covenants is that they are hierarchical. To put it another way, they are administered by His representatives who function according to a chain of command. God mediates His covenants through people. A hierarchy, simply defined, is an order that runs within a particular alignment.

Like automobiles that need to be properly aligned, covenants only work when they function in God's ordained order. The same wear and tear that shows up on tires when cars are out of alignment shows up in personal lives, marriages, families, churches, and societies when they ignore this vital component of a covenant. If you want to experience the provision and power of the covenant, you need to operate under the legitimate authority of the covenant.

We read in Genesis 1:26 that God said Adam and Eve were to rule over His creation. But that doesn't mean God abdicated His throne and turned everything over to mankind. Our authority to rule is under God, not apart from Him. God didn't say to Adam and Eve, "I made this for you. Rule it any way you want."

Adam and Eve were to rule, but not independently of the King. They were not to become autonomous. We live in a world today where men and women want autonomy. They want the right to rule apart from the One who is in charge.

In 1 Corinthians 11:3 Paul lays out this principle of God's hierarchical relationships in a much broader context: "I want you to understand that Christ is the head of every man, and the man is the head of a woman, and God is the head of Christ."

No person who names the name of Jesus Christ can claim autonomy. No man may say, "Because I am a man, I can do whatever I want." No, Christ is your head, your covering.

You are answerable to Him. We will look at 1 Corinthians 11 more fully in the section on family.

My point here is all of us are under authority. There is even a hierarchy in function within the equality of the Trinity because Paul said, "God is the head of Christ." That's why, when Jesus was on earth, He was obedient to the Father and said He would only do the Father's will. God works through a chain of command even within Himself in order to accomplish His plan and program in history.

Why is this so crucial? If you rebelliously break God's chain, you automatically lose His blessing and His covering. God's covenantal blessing flows through His authorized hierarchy. If you break off and do your own thing, become your own person, you forfeit the blessings God designed to flow down through His chain to you. You have rebelled against God's order.

Now you can see why Satan wants to mess up the roles God has assigned us. Satan went to Eve in the garden not because she was morally or intellectually weaker, but to bypass and distort Adam's headship.

Eve acted independently of Adam, and Adam failed to exercise his leadership. When Eve acted independently of her head and Adam refused to lead, roles were reversed, and Satan won.

This principle of representation is strong because the Bible says in 1 Corinthians 15:22 that "in Adam all die" (see also

Romans 5:12). Adam was our representative head, and when he fell, we all fell.

You may get upset and say, "I don't want Adam to represent me." You may not have voted for the president in the last election, but he can still send your sons and daughters to war because he is your representative. You may not agree with everything your senators do, but they still represent you in Congress.

But praise God, you have another representative whose name is Adam too. He is the "last Adam" (1 Corinthians 15:45), Jesus Christ, who reversed the effects of the first Adam's sin (Romans 5:21). When you decide to come under Jesus' representation, you share in His blessing. That's the principle of representation, which is at the heart of the hierarchical aspect of each of God's covenants. That's how God's covenant flows.

ETHICS

God's covenants are also ethically established. This is their third facet. By ethical I mean God's covenants have specific guidelines, or rules, that govern them. Let's go back to Genesis and the garden of Eden.

> Then the LORD God took the man and put him into the garden of Eden to cultivate it and keep it. And the

LORD God commanded the man, saying, "From any tree of the garden you may eat freely; but from the tree of the knowledge of good and evil you shall not eat, for in the day that you eat from it you shall surely die." (2:15–17)

God gave Adam a guideline to follow. God told him, "These are the rules of My kingdom. If you are going to reign here under Me, these are the rules you must obey. If you disobey My rules, you will suffer the consequences."

God has built a cause-effect relationship into His covenant rules. If you follow His rules, you get His benefits. If you follow your way, you lose His benefits and come under His penalties. When you operate under God's covenant rules, whatever the covenant is supposed to supply you with, it will supply.

This is why Satan wanted to deceive Adam and Eve. He knew if he could lead them to violate the covenant rules, they would lose the benefits and suffer God's penalty.

God told Joshua, "Be careful to do according to all the law which Moses My servant commanded you; do not turn from it to the right or to the left, *so that* you may have success wherever you go" (Joshua 1:7, italics added).

Joshua listened to what God told him. He and his leaders did what God told them, and Israel gained the Promised Land. But in the very next book of the Bible, the book of

Judges, the people failed to do what God said and suffered round after round of judgments.

What's true for a nation regarding a covenant is also true for an individual. When you rebel against the covenant's regulations, you lose because there is a cause-effect relationship. It has nothing to do with whether you like God's rules. It's not your kingdom. If you want to operate by your own rules, you need to go out and create your own world. But as long as you are in God's world, where God has set the rules, you must abide by His rules or you become a rebel against His kingdom government. And God always deals with rebels.

Suppose you go to the top of the Empire State Building and announce, "I don't like the rule of gravity. I'm not into gravity—never have been, never will be. Can't stand the thought of 'what goes up must come down.' Today I am going to rebel against the law of gravity. I am serving notice that this rule isn't going to tell me what to do."

So you stand on the top of the Empire State Building and do your Superman thing. You jump from the precipice and wave your fist in gravity's face.

As they sweep you off the pavement, it will become undeniably clear that whether you bought into gravity or not is irrelevant. The rule is the rule, and you will pay the price for trying to break it.

SANCTIONS

A fourth facet of God's covenants is sanctions. Covenants are attached to an oath, or pledge, that a person makes with regard to the agreement.

Whenever God establishes a covenant, the people who are entering it with Him must promise to obey and keep the covenant's stipulations. This pledge involves promises for obedience and penalties for disobedience. That's why the Bible says again and again that those who keep God's Word are the ones who are blessed (see James 1:25).

The oaths that accompany God's covenants are often called sanctions—those provisions that make a law binding. The clearest example of this process of oath-taking is in Deuteronomy 27–30, when Moses had the people of Israel stand between two mountains.

One was the mountain of blessing, and the other was the mountain of cursing. Moses read the blessings for keeping God's law and the curses for breaking it to the people, and the people said amen to signify they accepted and understood these terms. Then Moses said: "I have set before you life and death, the blessing and the curse. So choose life" (Deuteronomy 30:19).

We take many kinds of oaths today. Every morning, in schools across the country, kids stand and say, "I pledge allegiance to the flag . . ." That is an oath of allegiance.

When a believer comes to the water to be baptized, he or she is making a pledge, a statement of commitment to follow Jesus Christ. Baptism is an outward symbol of an inner reality. God's oaths often have symbols tied to them that are designed to reflect the intention of the oath.

The bottom line of a covenant oath is the same throughout Scripture. You are saying to God, "May good come upon me as I follow You, and may evil come upon me if I reject You."

INHERITANCE

Last, God's covenants have continuity and long-term, generational impact. What you do affects not only you; it affects those in contact with you and those who follow you. It has to do with inheritance.

Just ask Adam and Eve. Their sin spilled over into the next generation when Cain killed Abel, ultimately leading to worldwide judgment (see Genesis 6). Many people today are undergoing things they didn't have anything to do with personally. Their parents had everything to do with the problem, and their kids are suffering the repercussions of it.

A baby who is born addicted to alcohol or suffering from drug withdrawal needs medical treatment from the moment he leaves his mother's womb because someone else broke God's law.

Like all of God's principles, this one operates on the personal, familial, church, and civil level. I'm convinced the reason the blood of violence is flowing in our streets is that we are shedding innocent blood in America's abortion rooms (Proverbs 6:17). You cannot escape the repercussions of breaking God's law and inheriting the built-in consequences.

One reason you and I must fight to stay in God's will—and when we leave it, fight to get back in as quickly as possible—is life is not just about you and me. It includes many other people who will come after us.

In the Ten Commandments, God said He would pass the iniquity on to "the third and the fourth generations of those who hate Me" (Exodus 20:5). Even if you don't care for yourself, care for others because there are long-term consequences attached to the covenant. Break the cycle with you.

NEW COVENANT

In Scripture the word "testament" means "covenant." So when you read through the New Testament, you are actually reading about the new covenant. When Jesus Christ was preparing to die on the cross, He held a Communion service with His disciples. At that meal, He said, "This is My blood of the covenant, which is poured out for many for forgiveness of sins" (Matthew 26:28). In that statement Jesus wasn't just referring to the Passover. The Passover goes back to when God delivered Israel from Egypt and He told them to slay a lamb and place the blood of the lamb on the doorpost in order for the death angel to see the blood and pass over it.

When Jesus referenced His blood of the covenant, He meant so much more. We read about the new covenant in the book of Hebrews where it says,

> So much the more also Jesus has become the guarantee of *a better covenant.* The former priests, on the one hand, existed in greater numbers because they were prevented by death from continuing, but Jesus, on the other hand, because He continues forever, holds His priesthood permanently. Therefore He is able also to save forever those who draw near to God through Him, since He always lives to make intercession for them. (Hebrews 7:22–25, italics added)

When Jesus was on earth, His job description was to fulfill the law and pay for the sins of mankind on the cross. After He did that and rose from the dead, He is now seated at the right hand of the Father. Part of His job description in the New Covenant is to "make intercession" for the saints, which includes you.

This passage is being directed at Christians, not non-Christians, so when the term "save" is used, it is talking about "rescuing" rather than saving for eternity in heaven. Christ's full-time job under the new covenant is to intercede for, rescue, and deliver the saints. You are not on your own. You are not alone. If you come under the facets of the New Covenant, Jesus Christ is positioned to intercede for you, rescue you, and deliver you from whatever challenge you are facing.

But the only way to experience His saving power on a daily basis is to align yourself according to the facets of the covenant. If you choose to operate outside of the covenant, you are on your own and you won't experience the power, provision, protection, and authority that comes from the King. Understanding and living according to God's covenantal relationship is key to experiencing the abundant life He has promised to give to you.

CHAPTER FIVE

THE POWER

We conclude our time together by looking at the designations, or spheres, of God's kingdom as they relate to covenants, as well as how they relate to the areas of governance within God's established program. There are four basic covenantal spheres through which God's kingdom operates: personal, familial, church, and society. We are reviewing each of these four spheres in a brief way here; each of the four accompanying booklets in the *Life Under God* series goes into one particular sphere in depth (*One Life Under God, One Family Under God, One Church Under God, One Nation Under God*).

PERSONAL

The first sphere we need to deal with involves the individual. When you came to know Jesus Christ, you entered into a personal covenant with Him. You turned the government, the direction of your life, over to Him. Because you have entered into a personal relationship with Christ, when you stand before Him at the judgment seat it won't be a group meeting (2 Corinthians 5:10). Even unbelievers will have to give a personal account to God (Revelation 20:11–15).

One reason you should study God's Word and spend time with Him is to find out what the Governor of your life has to say to you. Philippians 2:12 and 13 are verses you need to read and memorize. Paul said, "Work out your salvation with fear and trembling; for it is God who is at work in you, both to will and to work for His good pleasure." Why are these verses so important to you as a kingdom citizen? Because you are personally responsible to God. This is one of those seminal passages for understanding the personal covenant the Lord has made with you, and the purpose He has for you in advancing His kingdom.

Notice first that you have something to do when it comes to discerning God's call. You can't live off what your mother or father did for the Lord. Nor can you live off of what your friends are doing. You are to "work out your own" growth. You need to find the calling of God for your life directly from Him.

Others can certainly help you in the process. Get all the information you can. But then you are to go on your face before God, asking Him to show you what He wants you to do. You cannot piggyback on another believer to find your calling. Notice what else Paul said here. Your work will not be in vain because God is also at work in you.

Paul was not talking about working to become a Christian. You can't work to become a Christian. But once you are saved by the grace of God, He works in you in order to work through you.

So you are at work, and God is at work. Your responsibility is to commit yourself to God and seek His will. You don't just wake up one morning and find your calling. You have to go through the process. But God meets you in the process. The implications of this are huge. It means we can't blame other people for our mess. Someone may say, "But you don't know what happened to me. You don't know how someone messed me up." That's true. I don't know what happened to you. But the issue is what are you going to do? Each of us needs to take personal responsibility for our lives and for how we respond to what others have done to us.

Self-governance means self-control of one's attitudes and actions apart from external coercion. Personal governance is the foundation for leadership and every other form of government, since those who cannot govern themselves cannot properly govern others.

God's ultimate goal for mankind is self-government under Him. Why? Because every believer will give an account to God individually. The Bible says in Romans 14:12, "Each one of us will give an account of himself to God."

Jesus said that at His return, "I will then repay every man according to his deeds" (Matthew 16:27). Peter also said each of us will give an account to God and be judged accordingly (see 1 Peter 4:5). In fact every man, including the unrighteous, will give an account to God (see Revelation 20:11–15).

When you stand before God, your family can't come along with you to support you. You can't call the elders or deacons at church to help you out. When you stand before God, you will not be able to call on the governor, the mayor, the city council, or anyone else to plead your case. You will stand alone before Christ to account for the way you governed your life under Him.

This is why I say that God's goal for our lives as individuals is always personal responsibility. If you are going to live life the way life was meant to be lived in God's kingdom, you must learn to govern your life according to His rules.

When you look at it from this standpoint, you can see that the other three spheres of government are also the three primary institutions God established in His Word to help produce proper self-government. The family, the church, and the civil government are all designed to play a special and unique role in producing proper self-government under God.

The family is not supposed to govern you all your life, but to raise and train you to govern yourself under God. The church is not supposed to run your life but to disciple you to govern yourself under God. And the civil government was certainly never designed to run your life, but to act as God's minister in providing conditions under which you can carry out good personal responsibility in a safe and productive manner.

Now you can see why, when people lose the ability to govern themselves, they mess up the institutions God has created to help them be self-governing.

If a husband and father won't govern himself, he is going to mess up his family. If members in a church don't govern themselves, there will be chaos in the congregation. And if the citizens in a society don't govern themselves, you can't hire enough policemen to fix the crime problem that results.

What we have done in this country is take the things God meant to be decentralized and make them the primary responsibility of civil government—thus creating chaos and confusion. For example, we centralized charity in the federal government and created a well-intentioned yet wasteful and dependent system called welfare. We have centralized one thing after another, so now we've got this huge bureaucracy the citizenry has to pay for through excessive taxation. If you ask the government to do it, you have to pay the government to do it.

This concept of self-government, or personal responsibility, is the cornerstone to the meaning and expression of true freedom.

FAMILY

The second sphere in God's kingdom is the family. It is God's foundation, the institutional building block for the rest of society. Malachi 2:14 calls marriage a covenant, and that covenant is expanded through the birth and rearing of children. The family was created to uniquely model God's Trinitarian character in history and proliferate His image throughout the world (see Genesis 1:26–28).

Genesis 18:19 is a very enlightening verse in this regard. God entered into a covenant with Abraham in which He said that Abraham was to raise his family according to God's commands so God could bring blessing to Abraham and his offspring.

Deuteronomy 6:1–9 is that great passage where God says He is the Lord and we are to teach our children about Him. Parents have the responsibility to get God's truth into the hearts and lives of their children, that His blessing might come to the children through their parents.

God told Adam about the trees of the garden before He created Eve (see Genesis 2:16–17), so Adam's job was to tell Eve what God had said. There was to be a transfer of information from the husband to the wife—then, when they became parents, to their children.

Women have a very important role to play in the family covenant. When God calls a woman a "helper" (Genesis 2:18), how is she supposed to help? She is supposed to help her husband fulfill God's calling on their home while simultaneously fulfilling her own calling. Together their family is to be stronger in advancing God's kingdom than they would be on their own.

I think of Moses and his wife, Zipporah, in Exodus 4:24–26—an unusual passage—as an example of this. God had told Moses the sign of His covenant for the males of Israel would be circumcision. But Moses had failed to circumcise his own son and the Bible says God sought to put Moses to death for his rebellion against the covenant.

But Zipporah, seeing the wrath of God against her husband, took a knife and quickly circumcised their son. She threw the foreskin at Moses' feet in disgust because his failure had jeopardized their family.

Rather than fussing, Zipporah acted. And her actions caused God to retract from His intention to kill Moses. Even though the husband failed in this situation, the wife took up the slack and the home was saved.

When a woman says, "My man isn't everything he is supposed to be," she needs to ask in addition, "Am I the helper God created me to be?" It may be through her that the family will be preserved.

When talking of the sphere of the family, an element of

governance comes into play. By family governance I am referring to the jurisdiction of authority whereby parents are responsible for their children and for how their family contributes to the other spheres of governance.

The church isn't responsible for your children. The church can help equip you and support you in raising your children, but you are responsible for your children. Neither is the government—or the school system—responsible for raising your children.

In biblical family governance, there used to be a time when it was clear the father was the head of this government. There used to be a time when it was understood that, like Joshua, a father's most important role was saying, "As for me and my house, we will serve the Lord" (Joshua 24:15).

Let me get specific. In biblical family government, the responsibility for educating children rested with the home. It was the duty of parents, not the state, to see to the education of their children and make sure they were raised in the "discipline and instruction of the Lord" (see Ephesians 6:4; compare with Deuteronomy 6:1–9). The only way parents can fulfill that command is to apply God's truth to every area of a child's life and education.

But when we turn the education of our children over to the state, and the state removes biblical ethics from its curriculum, what you get is the mess we have now. What we have now in education is information devoid of godly ethics. So instead of teaching the theory of evolution, the public school teaches the fact of evolution.

Once you tell the state, "I'm going to pay you to educate my children," the state can educate them according to the state's rules, not according to your rules. This becomes a misapplication of biblical authority and government.

Here is another one: In the Bible, economics and charity resided in the family. You could not go to the church for money until the church first asked, "Have you gone to your parents, siblings, or other relatives for help first?" (see 1 Timothy 5:4, 8).

You couldn't skip over your family and jump to the church. And you certainly couldn't skip over the family and the church and jump to the federal government and say, "It's payday. Hand me a check." That's not the way it was meant to be.

The family—with the father as president, the mother as vice president, and both raising the children—is to be the backbone of biblical society. That is why, when family government fails, woe is everything else because everything else is predicated on the family. The saga of a nation is the saga of its families written large.

That's not just theoretical. Read chapters 3–6 of Genesis and you'll see that sin, which started when Adam and Eve failed and Cain killed Abel, eventually poisoned the whole human race. God had to destroy the whole race because the failure of the family is the bottom-line cause of disintegration in the church and the government.

CHURCH

The third sphere in God's kingdom agenda is the church. In 1 Corinthians 11:25 Paul said the church is a new covenant. It is the new arrangement by which God relates to His kingdom people. The job of the church is to manifest the ethics of the kingdom before a watching world. Paul said this in the context of the Communion service, in which we are to sit in judgment of ourselves so God might not judge us (see 1 Corinthians 11:29–32).

We can't have it both ways. Paul also said, "You cannot drink the cup of the Lord and the cup of demons; you cannot partake of the table of the Lord and the table of demons" (1 Corinthians 10:21).

If you are going to be in God's kingdom where He rules, you must sit at His table. Don't try to have chairs at two different tables. Don't give God Sunday and give somebody else Monday through Saturday. He is our full-time Master. In the covenant of the church, our job is to disciple the saints to live for the kingdom.

The Bible also says in 1 Thessalonians 5:12–13 that church leaders have charge over the flock of God. In 1 Timothy 5:17 Paul said elders are responsible to rule. The author of Hebrews wrote that members of the church are to obey and submit to their spiritual leaders (Hebrews 13:17).

Mature, set-apart spiritual leaders are God's method of

ruling in His government of the church. The church is distinct from the family and from the civil government. It is a unique governmental rule under God.

The church's purpose is to equip you to live before God with proper self-government and family-government. The job of the church is not to solve all of your problems but to show you how to solve your problems under God. The church can assist you in doing that, but it cannot do it for you.

The church is the most important formal institution on earth. The church, and only the church, has been commissioned by the sovereign Lord to be His representative agency in history. It has been given sole authority to unlock the treasures of the spiritual realm so they can be brought to bear on the realities of earth; the church alone possesses the keys to the kingdom (Matthew 16:18,19).

God designed the church to be the epicenter of culture, and the church's strength or weakness is a major determining factor in the success or failure of human civilization. When the church is strong, the culture is impacted positively—even if the "powers that be" in a particular place don't realize that impact and seek to marginalize and persecute the church. But when the church is weak, its influence deteriorates and so does the culture.

One example of the church's impact, both positively and negatively, is the institution of slavery in America. Many segments of American culture condoned and sanctioned slavery, even though it served as the catalyst for a civil war that cost thousands of lives and helped produce ongoing cultural upheaval. Christendom at large helped provide justification for slavery, even leading some to find a basis for slavery in Scripture. But it was the strength of the true church bringing its influence to bear that helped lead to the collapse of slavery.

CIVIL GOVERNMENT

The fourth covenantal sphere is one that reaches beyond the individual, the family, and the church to the broadest structures of society, from the federal government to the local school board. Romans 13 sets out the parameters of this covenant. "Every person is to be in subjection to the governing authorities. For there is no authority except from God, and those which exist are established by God" (v. 1).

This is interesting, because the ruler when this passage was written was the Roman emperor Nero. God was saying, in a paraphrase, "Even pagan rulers only rule by My permission. And when I get tired of their pagan behavior, I will remove them."

Government is God's appointed representative. According to verse 2, if we resist the legitimate authority of government, we are "oppos[ing] the ordinance of God." We are not just fighting the government; we are fighting God.

I need to point out that what God authorizes in Romans 13

is the concept of governing authority, not necessarily every-thing a particular authority does. There must be a distinction.

People in a legitimate office can operate in illegitimate ways. We must oppose illegitimacy and evil no matter where they are found, but that does not negate God's establishment of government. You don't have to like the mayor or the president, but you must honor the offices of mayor and president.

The God-ordained purposes of civil government are to reward and promote good behavior and to restrain and punish evil behavior.

> Rulers are not a cause of fear for good behavior, but for evil. Do you want to have no fear of authority? Do what is good, and you will have praise from the same; for it is a minister of God to you for good. But if you do what is evil, be afraid; for it does not bear the sword for nothing. (vv. 3–4)

The government may not do its job very well, but God still gives government tremendous authority to carry out its assignment. When children stop being afraid of disobeying their parents, the home is in trouble. When members disrespect leadership, the church is in trouble. And when citizens don't respect the law of the land, the land is in trouble.

This is why people in many cities have burglar bars on their windows and triple locks on their doors. People no longer respect authority; they have no fear of God or of punishment. Government is God's plan to manage society. It is a legitimate covenant we have to recognize and submit ourselves to.

You can rebel against God's covenant if you want to, and for a while you may seem to get away with it. But in the Bible there is a fixed law that says, "Do not be deceived, God is not mocked; for whatever a man sows, this he will also reap" (Galatians 6:7). To put it another way, what you put in the soil, you're going to see again. If you plant corn, don't look for squash. If you plant okra, don't expect green beans.

You have a responsibility to the government you live under. The apostle Peter spelled it out:

> Submit yourselves for the Lord's sake to every human
> institution, whether to a king as the one in authority,
> or to governors as sent by him for the punishment of
> evildoers and the praise of those who do right. For
> such is the will of God that by doing right you may
> silence the ignorance of foolish men. (1 Peter 2:13–15)

Did you know civil government in the Bible was designed to be small, not large? Its reach was meant to be limited, not all-encompassing. In the Bible civil government is not the whole show. It is only one of three God-ordained institutions, along with the family and the church. Simply stated, the biblical role of civil government is to maintain a safe, just, and righteous environment for freedom to flourish.

Civil government is supposed to spend its time and energy removing tyranny from the marketplace and maintaining order in society—in other words, promoting and administering justice, protecting law-abiding citizens, and punishing the lawless.

Civil government is designed to make sure fairness operates in such areas as business and racial relationships. Government should see that men are not allowed to do evil and bring injustice into society.

The job of the civil government is to maintain justice, protect freedom, and defend its citizens. In Scripture, the government has virtually no authority in education, business, welfare, or ecclesiastical affairs, except to make sure there are no injustices and the market is free from tyranny and discrimination.

One of the biblical things the government did was to intervene in the injustices of racism and segregation in the South. That was a biblical role of government because injustice and tyranny were involved.

Each of God's governmental institutions has its own sphere of operation. The governing spheres of God's kingdom are not only decentralized, they are pluralized. They operate from the bottom up within specific areas of responsibility. This means all government begins with self-government. Each one of God's governing authorities cooperates and interconnects with the others without compromising jurisdictional boundaries in order to produce accountability, responsibility, and productivity at the lowest possible level. The individual should impact and strengthen the government of the family. The family should do likewise with the church, and the church should overflow to the enhancement of every institution in society.

This is how God's kingdom operates: through decentralized, plural institutions under His centralized leadership, in order to produce self-government under Him.

God's kingdom agenda also works so that it balances love and discipline. Hebrews 12:6 says God loves us but He disciplines us. Parents are to love their children enough to discipline them (see Ephesians 6:4).

The civil government is to honor and praise people who do what is right (see Romans 13:3). But the government also has the responsibility to discipline and judge citizens who break the law (see v. 4).

All of God's institutions marry love with discipline. The method of discipline for the family is the rod. The method of discipline for the church is the Communion table, accountability, and excommunication. The method of discipline for the government is imprisonment, corporal, and capital punishment. God has given each governmental institution a disciplining mechanism that people might be led to self-government under Him or else suffer the appropriate consequences.

THE BLESSINGS OF THE KINGDOM

God's kingdom agenda operates to bring His blessing to the institutions that follow it.

In Deuteronomy 29:9, Moses told Israel, "Keep the words of this covenant to do them, that you may prosper in all that you do." The Scripture is simply saying that if you do it God's way, you'll see the benefits.

America attempted to do this in its early days. The effort was flawed because of unbiblical slavery, but apart from slavery this country attempted to operate by a decentralized government. And we prospered like no country in the history of mankind, even though not everybody at the top was a Christian.

In 3 John 2, the apostle prays Gaius would prosper "in all respects" just as he prospered in his spiritual life. John is saying the same thing. If you do things God's way, benefit comes. And the benefit flows over into the family, the church, and the government.

This progression of blessing is laid out beautifully in my favorite Psalm, Psalm 128. In verses 1–2 we see the blessing that comes from personal responsibility or self-government: "How blessed is everyone who fears the LORD, Who walks in His ways. When you shall eat of the fruit of your hands, you will be happy and it will be well with you."

Then the blessing moves to the family: "Your wife shall

be like a fruitful vine Within your house, Your children like olive plants Around your table" (v. 3). When you become responsible for yourself, your mate, and your children flourish.

Next in line is the church. "The LORD bless you from Zion" (Psalm 128:5). Zion was the place of worship where the temple was located. The church—the people of God, the spiritual community—is blessed when God's government operates the way it should, since it is the New Testament expression of Zion (see Hebrews 12:22–24).

What happens when the individual, the family, and the church get it right? The government of the nation experiences blessing: "May you see the prosperity of Jerusalem all the days of your life. Indeed, may you see your children's children. Peace be upon Israel!" (Psalm 128:5b–6).

When people govern themselves under God, you have peace and blessing. When people look to everything and everyone else to govern them except God, you have anarchy. God has established His kingdom to function in a way that benefits those aligned under it.

When we follow God's rules, honor Christ as Lord, come under His covenantal covering, and respect the governing guidelines, we will benefit from the power, authority, blessings, provision, and protection of our great King.

THE URBAN
ALTERNATIVE

D r. Tony Evans and The Urban Alternative (TUA) equips, empowers, and unites Christians to impact individuals, families, churches, and communities to restore hope and transform lives.

We believe the core cause of the problems we face in our personal lives, homes, churches, and societies is a spiritual one; therefore, the only way to address them is spiritually. We've tried a political, a social, an economic, and even a religious agenda. It's time for a Kingdom Agenda—God's visible and comprehensive rule over every area of life—because when we function as we were designed, there is a divine power that changes everything. It renews and restores as the life of Christ is made manifest within our own. As we align ourselves under Him, there is an alignment that happens from deep within—where He brings about full restoration. It is an atmosphere that revives and makes whole.

As it impacts us, it impacts others—transforming every sphere of life in which we live. When each biblical sphere of life functions in accordance with God's Word, the outcomes are evangelism, discipleship, and community impact. As we learn how to govern ourselves under God, we then transform the institutions of family, church, and society from a biblically based kingdom perspective. Where through Him, we are touching heaven and changing earth.

To achieve our goal we use a variety of strategies, methods, and resources for reaching and equipping as many people as possible.

BROADCAST MEDIA

Hundreds of thousands of individuals experience *The Alternative with Dr. Tony Evans* through the daily radio broadcast playing on nearly 1,000 radio outlets and in over 130 countries. The broadcast can also be seen on several television networks and is viewable online at TonyEvans.org.

LEADERSHIP TRAINING

The Kingdom Agenda Pastors (KAP) provides a *viable network* for *like-minded pastors* who embrace the Kingdom Agenda philosophy. Pastors have the opportunity to go deeper with Dr. Tony Evans as they are given greater biblical knowledge, practical applications, and resources to impact individuals, families, churches, and communities. KAP welcomes *senior and associate pastors* of all churches.

The Kingdom Agenda Pastors' Summit progressively develops church leaders to meet the demands of the 21st century while maintaining the Gospel message and the strategic position of the church. The Summit introduces *intensive seminars, workshops,* and *resources*, addressing issues affecting the community, family, leadership, organizational health, and more.

Pastors' Wives Ministry, founded by Dr. Lois Evans, provides *counsel, encouragement,* and *spiritual resources* for pastors' wives as they serve with their husbands in the ministry. A primary focus of the ministry is the KAP Summit that offers senior pastors' wives a safe place to *reflect, renew,* and *relax* along with training in personal development, spiritual growth, and care for their emotional and physical well-being.

COMMUNITY IMPACT

National Church Adopt-A-School Initiative (NCAASI) prepares churches across the country to impact communities by using *public schools as the primary vehicle for effecting positive social change* in urban youth and families. Leaders of churches, school districts, faith-based organizations, and other nonprofit organizations are equipped with the knowledge and tools to *forge partnerships* and build *strong social service delivery systems.* This training is based on the comprehensive church-based community impact strategy conducted by Oak Cliff Bible Fellowship. It addresses such areas as economic development, education, housing, health revitalization, family renewal, and racial reconciliation. We also assist churches in tailoring the model to meet the specific needs of their communities while simultaneously addressing the spiritual and moral frame of reference.

RESOURCE DEVELOPMENT

We are fostering lifelong learning partnerships with the people we serve by providing a variety of published materials. We offer booklets, Bible studies, books, CDs, and DVDs to strengthen people in their walk with God and ministry to others.

* * *

For more information, a catalog of Dr. Tony Evans'
ministry resources, and a complimentary copy of
Dr. Evans' devotional newsletter,
call (800) 800-3222,
or write TUA at P.O. Box 4000, Dallas TX 75208,
or log on to
TonyEvans.org.

COMPLETE YOUR

DR. TONY EVANS

LIBRARY

IN THE KINGDOM AGENDA SERIES,

Dr. Tony Evans offers inexpensive resources which explore
God's intentions for life. Through masterful illustrations,
church members learn how to give sacrificially, thrive in
their marriages & activate the power of the cross.

MORE INFORMATION AVAILABLE AT THEKINGDOMAGENDABOOK.COM

MOODY
Publishers™

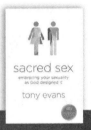

ORE INFORMATION AVAILABLE AT THEKINGDOMAGENDABOOK.COM

MOODY
Publishers™

The Life Under God Series

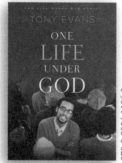

978-0-8024-1186-0

978-0-8024-1141-9

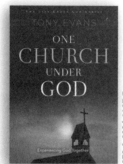

978-0-8024-1187-7

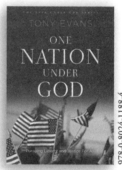

978-0-8024-1188-4

God's Word offers a biblically based kingdom agenda.
In The Life Under God series, Dr. Tony Evans highlights the four
areas which God has entrusted to us—personal, family, church,
and society—and demonstrates that Scripture has provided a clear
authority and a comprehensive approach to all of life.

MORE INFORMATION AVAILABLE AT THEKINGDOMAGENDABOOK.COM

MOODY Publishers™